Growing Your Business with Search Engines,
Social Media and Content Marketing

FOUND

Connecting with Customers
in the Digital Age

Matthew W. Certo

FOUND

Connecting with Customers
in the Digital Age

Matthew W. Certo

ISBN: 061596222X
ISBN 13: 9780615962221

To my late friend, Isaac Hunter.

ABOUT THE AUTHOR

Matt Certo serves as CEO and Principal of Findsome & Winmore, an Orlando, Florida-based digital marketing agency. Originally called WebSolvers, the company's first client was his alma mater, Rollins College. Nearly twenty years ago, he built the college's first website out of his dorm room at the age of nineteen.

Since then, Matt has grown the company into a fully integrated digital marketing agency with experienced professionals, a diverse client base, and an ever-increasing suite of services dedicated to helping clients find and win new customers. Apart from the growth of the company, Certo's work in the industry has been extensive: he coauthored a book in 2001 (*Digital Dimensioning: Finding the ebusiness in Your Business*) and was asked by the White House to speak on digital trends at a domestic economic forum hosted by President George W. Bush.

Certo has also conceived and overseen a number of software products that are in widespread use today. He is a frequent guest speaker on topics that include marketing, web strategy, and search engine optimization, an area for which he has also served as a testifying expert witness. His clients have included the likes of Darden Restaurants, Newman's Own Organics, National Retail Properties, Fiserv, and McGraw-Hill. He is a frequent guest speaker to various marketing, advertising, and public relations trade associations and has been widely quoted in publications including *The Huffington Post, The San Diego Union Tribune, The Boston Globe* and *The Orlando Sentinel.*

An active community leader, Matt has served as board chairman of a number of nonprofit organizations including Ronald McDonald House Charities of Central Florida and The First Tee of Central Florida, an organization he founded. He has also served for nearly a decade on the board of the Edyth Bush Charitable Foundation as well as chairman of its endowment committee. He has been recognized by the *Orlando Business Journal* as one of its "Most Influential Men to Watch" and has appeared on its "40 Under 40 list" three times.

E-mail: mcerto@findsomewinmore.com
Twitter: @mcerto

ADVANCE PRAISE FOR FOUND

After reading *Found*, my digital IQ increased significantly. I'm more confident interacting with our Digital team and more committed to funding our Digital efforts.

Eugene Lee
President and Chief Operating Officer
Darden Restaurants (NYSE:DRI)

Certo has been helping clients develop successful digital marketing strategies since I met him in the late 1990s. *Found* provides you with detailed practical advice on how to do it in your own business.

W. Earl Sasser
Baker Foundation Professor
Harvard Business School

Found is a guidebook that every CEO should read. Matt Certo lays out a step-by-step process to identify and capture customers in the social marketing era.

Julian E. (Jay) Whitehurst
President and COO
National Retail Properties (NYSE:NNN)

Found brilliantly captures the challenges and opportunities in digital marketing today—getting this right is the x-factor in the success or failure of a business. Kudos to Matt Certo for capturing the essence of the problem and applying real-world recommendations for how to be remarkable in our hyperconnected universe.

Lori Wright
Chief Marketing Officer
TIBCO (NASD:TIBX)

ACKNOWLEDGMENTS

Writing a book is a lengthy journey and it cannot be taken alone. I would like to thank some of the people who have helped me to make this book a reality.

For starters, I would like to thank my teammates at Findsome & Winmore, a special family that has both contributed to the ideas in this book and supported me in its development. I especially wish to thank my fellow principals, Kelly Lafferman and Rich Wahl, for their encouragement. I would also like to thank Kelly Rogers for her ongoing support of this work.

I also want to acknowledge the many friends and colleagues who agreed to review this manuscript during its development and to offer both constructive criticism and encouragement. One of those reviewers, Jay Whitehurst, took a particularly strong interest in this work and helped me substantially. I would also like to thank Guy Kawasaki for writing *APE: Author, Publisher, Entrepreneur*. His book was most helpful to me in starting, continuing, and finishing this project.

Lastly, I would like to thank my entire family, whose ongoing love and support is so important to me. I most certainly could not have reached the finish line without their encouragement.

TABLE OF CONTENTS

PREFACE

What new technology does is create new opportunities to do a job that customers want done.

—Tim O'Reilly

Let me offer you a hypothetical situation. Suppose you are sitting in a crowded theater waiting for a movie to begin. Right before the lights go down, a man calmly walks to the front of the room. He is holding a parachute and announces that this product is on sale for one hundred dollars. What's more, he tells you that he has plenty in stock.

Would you be interested in buying a parachute from this man? Probably not. In fact, you would probably be both confused and annoyed. The offer is irrelevant, out of context, and ill timed. You came to see a movie, not to hear a sales pitch.

But now imagine that you are sitting on a cross-country flight with two hundred strangers when the pilot comes on the intercom and says the following:

Ladies and gentlemen, good afternoon from the flight deck. My name is Captain Rogers. We're presently cruising at about thirty-two thousand feet, the skies are clear and smooth, and we are about fifteen minutes ahead of schedule.

That said, we have a major mechanical problem and won't be able to land. Unfortunately, I'm afraid this plane is going down. I'm so sorry for the trouble, but we have no Plan B and no parachutes on board. You're welcome to jump if you'd like, but that sure is a heck of a drop.

In the meantime, your flight attendants will be making their way through the cabin to collect all your empty cups and glasses. We know you have a choice when you fly, so we want to thank you for choosing our airline.

Right after he signs off, you realize that the same parachute salesman is sitting in the front row. He calmly unbuckles his seat belt, stands up to face the passengers, and gives the same pitch that he did in the theater: parachutes on sale for one hundred dollars.

Would you be more interested in this offer? Of course you would. We all would.

Admittedly, this scenario is a bit extreme if not ridiculous. But it illustrates the primary premise of this book: *the degree to which people are interested in buying your products fluctuates over time.* And in order to connect with your customers, you must do so at the *right* time—a point exacerbated in the age of Google, Facebook, and the smartphone. In short, a marketer's behavior must change.

While consumers may be annoyed by your messages at certain times, they can be downright desperate for them at others. The key to selling more is connecting with them at those "right" times. The goal of this book is to help you identify and take advantage of those points in time when your customers most desperately need your product—those "parachute moments"—and spend your energy there.

What are Parachute Moments?

Parachute moments are those points in time when your customers most desperately need your product.

In order to identify these moments, it is critical to understand the impact of technology on this process. The arrival and evolution of technologies such as the iPhone, Google, and Facebook have made these parachute moments more identifiable than ever. Using display advertising is the equivalent of selling a parachute to an audience in a movie theater. We can liken search marketing, on the other hand, to selling the same product to the passengers on the airplane in crisis.

As consumers, we get our news from Facebook, search Google for pretty much everything, and browse our iPads while watching television—leaving a digital trail the whole time. These behaviors leave clues behind, and these clues can guide your efforts to insert your brand into the equation. This book is about how brands can realign themselves to take advantage of the nature of this shifting tide—not to drown in it.

This book is divided into three parts. In Part 1 we examine this shifting landscape to better acquaint readers with how the influx of devices and social networks has changed consumer behavior, and how content—not advertising—is the key to developing relationships with them. Part 2 of this book presents marketers and business owners with a framework for how to adjust to the new landscape, the primary steps of which include studying your audience, developing content, negotiating search engines, and engaging with social media. Finally, in Part 3, we discuss how to take these ideas forward within your company, and how to circumvent some all-too-familiar organizational barriers that tend to impede progress.

Over the last two decades I have worked with hundreds of truly gifted clients—CEOs, business owners, and marketers—who have aimed to achieve some sort of digital marketing success. Their inquisitiveness about how to do so has served as my primary inspiration for this book. As time has passed and technologies have come and gone, most of my clients have wanted the same simple thing: to acquire more customers using the promise of online technology. In other words, they wanted to reap the rewards that they keep reading about.

While working with so many of my clients, I've seen some trends and patterns emerge that I believe are worth sharing. It is my hope that this book not only helps you to better detect when your customers need you most, but also to better position your brand to be right there at that moment—to be *Found* by customers when they are ready to buy.

PART 1:
LANDSCAPE SHIFT

> Toto, I've a feeling we're not in Kansas any more.
> —Dorothy, *The Wizard of Oz*

Just a handful of years ago, Twitter, Instagram, and Pinterest did not exist. Now they are a mainstream part of our culture and affect our interactions with each other and the various brands that we patronize. We all depend on our smartphones and tablets to do everything from making a restaurant reservation to depositing a check. We are videoconferencing with one another—wirelessly—from a device that can fit inside a shirt pocket. The future that we have always talked about has arrived. Everything has changed.

THE "ALWAYS ON" CONSUMER

> The cell phone has become the adult's transitional object, replacing the toddler's teddy bear for comfort and a sense of belonging.
>
> —Margaret Heffernan

Always On

The next time you are driving or riding in a car and come to an intersection, take a minute to look at the drivers in the cars around yours. You'll likely see what I see: distracted drivers steering the wheel while talking, texting, or checking Facebook on their smartphones. If you do the same exercise in a movie theater or at a football game, you'll likely see the same thing.

Even pedestrians suffer the same affliction, to their own physical detriment. According to a study in the journal *Accident Analysis & Prevention*, accidents from walking and texting have resulted in 1,500 hospitalizations in a recent twelve-month period. We're dependent on, tethered to, reliant on, and addicted to our phones.

Not convinced? I was blown away recently to learn about the emerging phenomenon of "sleep texting." Dr. Elizabeth Dowdell, professor of nursing at Villanova University, has compiled anecdotal evidence and survey data that says nearly a third of respondents admitted to sending text messages while sleeping. Yes, *texting while sleeping.*

In the book entitled *Focus,* author and psychologist Daniel Goleman characterizes this overarching cultural trend as "life immersed in digital distraction [which] creates a near-constant cognitive overload." But *Found* is not meant to be a psychology text or a cultural commentary. My aim is not to speak to the societal implications of all this device attachment. Instead, it's to state the reality of the situation so that we might deal with it as marketers: whether we are talking on the phone or replying to a text, our devices are seemingly always powered up and connected. We're "always on."

Meet Jane

A friend of mine, a pediatrician, once invited me to lunch to talk about a frustration in his business. As we sat down to eat, he immediately started lamenting a recent drop in his business and the apparent rise of a competitor. According to him, young moms—his primary target—were taking their children to his competitors and not to him. After years of steady gains, he was experiencing a decline.

My friend did have an inkling of why this competitor was doing so well, which is why he invited me to lunch. "He's first on the list every time I run a Google search, and he's all over Facebook," reported my friend. By contrast, my frustrated lunch partner had little or no presence on social media and had an outdated website that hadn't been updated in over eighteen months.

While I listened to him talk, I began to form an image in my mind of his end customer in the context of the "always on" landscape shift. And when I began to talk to him about the decline he was seeing in his business, I started describing this image, and I even gave her a name: Jane. I told my friend that Jane, his customer, was different from the moms of just five or ten years ago. Tongue in cheek, here is how I described her:

- Jane is addicted to social media, and admits it.
- She checks Facebook throughout the day—even at stoplights. She posts pictures of her two kids

whenever they are caught doing something "super cute."

- Jane Googles everything.
- Once she's caught up with Facebook and Google, she checks out Instagram to see what she's missed, and who has (and hasn't) "liked" her photos.
- When Jane watches TV at night (assuming she has time), she uses Pinterest to get home decorating ideas.
- Every January, Jane takes her family copy of the *Yellow Pages* right from the front porch to the recycling bin.
- When Jane wants to buy something or take a trip, she searches for reviews on Yelp, TripAdvisor, or Amazon. Jane doesn't have a travel agent. In fact, she doesn't know what a travel agent is.
- When Jane needs a service person to work inside her home, she asks for a referral on Facebook instead of using the phone book, which she does not have.

To hammer home this point, our creative team developed a simple illustration to paint a picture of Jane, even going so far as to describe her as aloof with respect to her vendor relationships of choice, as seen below.

MEET JANE

She is married with three kids, a dog,
and manages her life on her smartphone.

Jane

Jane has friends.

She's addicted to
Social Media and admits it.
She checks Facebook
throughout the day and
while cooking dinner.
Once she's caught up,
she checks out Instagram
and uses Pinterest and
Twitter in front of the TV.
She is influenced by her
friends and family.

Jane Googles EVERYTHING!

She recycles the
Yellow Pages every year without
even opening them and
doesn't like ads in general.
When Jane wants an answer,
she wants it now
(Jane is high maintenance).

Jane is Scary Smart.

She takes her time
making a buying
decision because she
doesn't have time to
make a bad one. She
researches prices on
her phone and compares
different brands and
service providers on the fly.

Understanding the nuances of your customers is critical when you're trying to connect with them. The age of "always on" makes this all the more important.

I could have gone on and on about Jane, but I thought I'd made my point. My friend's typical buyer was now behaving differently. When she was in need of his service, someone else was being *Found*, instead of him. Why? Because his marketing efforts weren't in sync with how the buyers of today think and act.

While not all of your buyers will be young mothers on the go, Jane's portrait can be quite helpful to us. As you think about your particular group of buyers, it is important to look at them through the lens of "always on." This framework not only helps us understand Jane, but also her husband, kids, parents, and friends. These days, online and mobile device preoccupation knows no age or gender bias.

I Want It Now.

The devices and technologies are important, but it is also important to think about how this new era of hyperconnectivity has impacted our personalities and expectations. It probably goes without saying, but implicit in our hyperconnectedness is an expectation of immediacy. Google has conditioned us to expect information very quickly, if not instantly. I just searched for "Superman" on Google, and I received 188,000,000 listings in 0.35 seconds. That is too fast to fathom.

After years of using search engines, we barely think about how fast it all happens and how spoiled we have become. We simply expect fast answers to our questions, and we like to click the REFRESH button while we wait for an update. Consumers in the image of Jane don't like to wait. They want their answer, their offer, their recommendation *now*.

I Want It Free.

Beyond wanting it now, there is a much lower expectation that a consumer should have to pay for things. If you think about it, so much of what we can find online is free. I can take an online course from Yale University for free. I can read most of the *New York Times* for free. I can watch an instructional video on how to fix my faucet for free. The list goes on.

> Free is really, you know, the gift of Silicon Valley to the world.
>
> --Chris Anderson

This paradigm shift is mostly due to the arrival of the Internet and related technologies like the cloud—the notion of storing our digital lives online and accessing them from different devices through wireless Internet connections. Chris Anderson, Gerald Loeb Award–winning author and former editor of *WIRED* magazine, wrote a best-selling book about this concept called *Free: The Future of a Radical Price.* He characterizes this new expectation of free as "the gift of Silicon Valley to the world." And while I'm not sure the newspaper and magazine industries would agree that this was a "gift," most consumers certainly would.

One of our firm's longstanding clients is *Global Golf Post*, a weekly golf newsmagazine that delivers premium, original news content to nearly a million subscribers around the world. It is the first publication of its kind, and it is absolutely free. Five short years ago, it did not exist. Fast-forward to today, and it is perhaps the most widely read and influential publication in its industry, claiming prominent advertisers such as Titleist, Nike, FootJoy, and Rolex, and partnerships with many of the sport's most influential governing bodies. All of this has transpired while *Global Golf Post*'s traditional competitors have suffered dramatic declines in paid circulation.

> If we couldn't figure out a way to deliver this product to our customers for free, we knew that someone else would.
>
> --Jim Nugent, Founder, Global Golf Post

The *Post*'s founder and publisher, Jim Nugent, developed the vision for this venture five years ago, after running traditional golf publications for over twenty years. "Free," he says, "was then the emerging model for consumers. If we couldn't figure out a way to deliver this product to our customers for free, we knew that someone else would." Jim knew then what most of us know now—the Internet demands *free*.

There is a common reluctance to give meaningful things away for free when you are trying to generate revenue. But consider an interesting example from Geek Squad, the company that installs and fixes computers, televisions, and other electronic devices for consumers.

> "Our best customers are the people that think they can fix it themselves."
>
> --Robert Stephens, Founder, The Geek Squad

The company is a big believer in providing free instructional videos to consumers online. Ironically, these videos explain how to solve problems that the company normally charges for. Doesn't this undermine the company's revenue? According to Robert Stephens, Geek Squad founder, the opposite actually occurs: "Our best customers are the people that think they can fix it themselves," he explains. Presumably, informative and influential content brings users closer to the brand—not further away. And then they buy.

I'm Moving on to Something Else

High speed and zero cost have become the prices of admission for those wanting to capture the consumer's attention. And our attention is divided enough, as we know from those of us who insist on walking, driving, and sleeping while texting. But what is the message for brands?

Anecdotally, we might presume that the consumer who is not quickly satisfied will simply keep looking—and quickly. My image of Jane suggests an attitude and disposition—not of her own making—of a person who likes to solve problems and move on. Research data reinforces this premise.

Jakob Nielsen, perhaps the foremost thinker in this area of digital attention, concluded the following in a recent study:

Users often leave Web pages in 10–20 seconds, but pages with a clear value proposition can hold people's attention for much longer...

If you stop and think for a moment about your own experiences searching the Internet for answers, I would guess that your feelings would be similar. When you are in search of a quick answer or a solution to a problem, you have come to expect that the process will happen quickly and efficiently.

Overall, the takeaways for brands from consumers like Jane are clear: *I don't have a ton of time. Give me what I want (a) now, and (b) don't charge me for it. And if I can't find it, I will move on, because I know I can find it elsewhere. I'll just keep looking.*

Do You Accept This Shift?

I'm always sheepish about this question when I speak with clients, but it is an important one. Do you buy into the idea that the advent of these devices, connectivity, and apps have changed the way that consumers buy?

While it is hard to disagree with the emergence of these tools, it is hard for some to admit that it matters to their business. I can tell you unequivocally that it does. So if you think that these changes are important to your business, then the next step is to get your arms around this and formulate an approach. While doing so may seem a bit overwhelming, the good news is that the framework that the remainder of this book lays out will help you chart a pragmatic course. The *better* news is that you just might catch your competitors napping. After all, Jane is going to buy from *someone* and it might as well be you!

CONTENT MARKETING FUNDAMENTALS

> We are drowning in information but starved for knowledge.
>
> —John Naisbitt

The Hunters and the Hunted

We previously used a parachute to illustrate the dilemma of trying to sell a product under two different scenarios. The first example was *(a) when you were about to watch a movie and had absolutely no need for a parachute,* and the second was *(b) when you were in an airborne plane about to crash, never wanting anything more in your life.* It is easy to see the difference. We will use this as a springboard for understanding these particular moments within your own customer base.

The parachute illustration frames customers in two very different postures. In scenario (a), the customer is in the position of being hunted by a sales or marketing thrust. The sales and marketing effort takes a product and makes a wild guess that one person in a large pool of people might need or want it.

Along the way, the sales and marketing tactic *interrupts* the customers from some other activity and hopes to distract their attention for just long enough. Marketers use interruptions all the time—television commercials, sales calls, ads, Facebook ads, and more—to win you over. There can be some success with this, but you need lots of money and luck to pay for enough ads to catch enough people at the right time and convince them to buy. Author Seth Godin introduced most of us to this concept in 1999 in his book *Permission Marketing,* by calling this approach "interruption marketing."

Scenario (b) flips the former on its head. It seeks to isolate those times when users don't have to be interrupted because they are already seeking your service and need it more than ever. They use Google to find a quick answer to their questions, or they ask their Facebook friends for an online referral. They are looking for an answer now, and the one who delivers, wins. You don't have to time it right (the circumstances do that all on their own), and, if you play your cards right, you don't have to pay for the conversation like you do with an ad.

In essence, the customer goes from being the *hunted* (i.e., interrupted and annoyed) to being the *hunter.* You don't have to look for the customers; they ultimately come to you and give you the consent to begin building a relationship. If they don't immediately buy, they most certainly are great candidates to "like" you on Facebook, subscribe to your e-mail newsletter, or all of the above. Google famously dubbed this type of watershed/parachute moment as the Zero Moment of Truth.

> Everybody likes to buy, but no one likes to be sold.
>
> --Marketing Adage

From my years as an advisor to companies that deployed many online marketing techniques, it is my strong conviction that customers prefer to be hunters rather than the hunted. Author David Meerman Scott characterizes this marketing approach as "earning their way in" with customers. Said another way: not many of us like to be pursued and sold. Perhaps you are familiar with the saying that "everybody likes to buy, but no one likes to be sold." While that is not a particularly original conclusion, I rarely see companies truly come to terms with this truth and adapt accordingly, especially in the face of the digital landscape shift. Further, I have observed that *content* is the currency of this new marketplace, and its eventual payback is to enable brands to be *Found.*

What Is Content Marketing?

Content marketing is a marketing approach that seems to get less attention than social media marketing, online marketing, or even search marketing. When I talk to business owners about content marketing, it doesn't seem to get the recognition and head-nodding that others do. Content marketing is defined as the creation and distribution of content that informs and influences a particular audience, but does not advertise or sell.

In this respect, the brand becomes a publisher rather than a salesman. To Linda Boff, executive director of global digital marketing for GE, this approach "helps people relate to what it is we do, not what we sell." To Michael Brenner, vice president of marketing for SAP, content marketing is the "hottest trend in marketing because it is the biggest gap between what buyers want and what brands produce." From time to time you may hear the term *inbound marketing* (coined by HubSpot cofounder Brian Halligan) used interchangeably with content marketing because the content draws customers *toward* brands via search engines instead of the other way around.

What is Content Marketing?

Content marketing is defined as the creation and distribution of content that *informs* and *influences* a particular audience, but does not *advertise* or *sell.*

For a company like Target, the chain of retail and on-line big-box stores, the primary objective of its content marketing strategy is to drive traffic, not sales. Target created an online blog called *A Bullseye View*, which goes behind the scenes of the company and provides useful content for consumers. In a CMO.com interview discussing its content strategy, Dustee Jenkins, vice president of public relations for Target, said that the company does not produce content to sell products, but produces content *around* the products. While you might see an article on "Ten Tips for Flu Season" that inadvertently supports a line of products, you will rarely see pieces on the products themselves.

There are many other definitions of content marketing, but the common threads to most of them are information, education, and product alignment.

Examples of Early Content Marketing

Content marketing may be less popular a term than search marketing and social media marketing, but it certainly is not a new tactic. Looking at some early examples of content marketing not only serves to demonstrate its longevity, but also helps us to understand it in practice.

One of the first and earliest examples of content marketing was by John Deere, the iconic farm and landscaping equipment company founded in 1837. Starting in 1895, the company began publishing a newsmagazine for farmers called *Furrow* and distributed it to customers and prospects free of charge on behalf of its dealers. The magazine's early tagline was, "A journal of practical information devoted to the interests of better farming." An early cover of the magazine said, "Sent to you with the compliments of your John Deere Dealer."

Content Marketing is Not New

In 1904, Jell-O started arming its door-to-door salesmen with free cookbooks.

Beyond that, you would be hard-pressed to know that John Deere produced and distributed the magazine. Instead of ads, the publication focused on editorial content about farming challenges and trends, as well as commentaries and columns about the farming lifestyle.

It is clear from reviewing early issues that the focus was on informative content rather than sales promotion. Individual pieces included farming history, scientific observations, humor, and peer insights. Along the way, the John Deere name was quietly present, building loyalty and brand association. Today, the publication still exists and has been modernized with a tablet edition.

A similar example comes from Jell-O, which began implementing content marketing tactics around the turn of the twentieth century. In 1904, Jell-O started arming its door-to-door salesmen with free cookbooks. The "cookbooks" were actually small booklets conveniently sized for a kitchen recipe box. The booklets contained a wealth of recipes and included some subtle branding. Not surprisingly, the recipes in the cookbooks used a fair amount of Jell-O, but the tactic was quite discernible: inform, inspire, and educate your customers, and the product or brand will naturally become a part of the conversation. As you can probably imagine, Jell-O (and Kraft Foods, its parent company), continues this tradition today online in its many websites and social media channels such as Pinterest, Facebook, and YouTube.

Content Marketing in Today's Marketplace

Using these examples as a guide, you can see contemporary content marketing examples everywhere—both online and print. I recently attended a conference in Los Angeles that was held at an upscale hotel. In the room was a copy of a new magazine called *BEYOND: A Journal on Design and Craftsmanship*. The publication had a very well-made "feel" to it, with rustic colors and imagery, and paper that was much thicker and more durable than your typical magazine.

As I flipped through the pages, I found interesting articles on craftsmanship and artisanal pursuits, as well as gift ideas that seemed to be produced by accomplished designers. It didn't take long, though, to recognize that the Lexus automobile brand was front and center as the publisher, along with some content about Lexus design innovations.

The magazine itself was free, and it presumably had an intended distribution to executives who might stay in that hotel. This is exactly the audience that Lexus is after. But the magazine was not an advertisement, and it certainly did not try to sell me anything. It was simply an example of a brand creating informative, original content with the intent of positioning the Lexus brand within it.

A more visible, online example of this is the American Express OPEN Forum, a marketing initiative of American Express that has really become a movement more than a tactic. The OPEN Forum is a community, content library, and social media companion that educates the small business owner on matters such as cash flow, legal matters, and human resources policies.

If you take a stroll through the OPEN Forum's Twitter feed, you will see informative, original articles on things such as internship policies, elevating your online shopping experience, and the pros and cons of sitting at work—all in an afternoon. American Express publishes hardback books on topics such as online marketing (which they distribute for free), and developed an online peer network where small business owners can share ideas and ask each other for advice. All the while, the brand is in the background, reinforcing the high image of American Express and keeping it in your mind for future financial decisions. However, never once does American Express "yell" at me to upgrade my card or buy an add-on.

This type of approach demonstrates how giving away content is an emerging trend with AmEx. Why is it important? According to Walter Frye, an American Express marketing director, "Content is an important piece in all of our marketing efforts...Extending our messaging through content is a great way for us to continue to convert our customers from simply seeing a message to considering our brand."

> Content is an important piece in all of our marketing efforts... Extending our message through content is a great way for us to continue to convert our customers from simply seeing a message to considering our brand.
>
> --Walter Frye, Marketing Director,
> American Express

To grasp the contrast, consider this approach against the dozens of credit card offers and solicitations you receive in the mail and at airports. Which approach makes you feel closer and more trusting, in terms of the brand? Which one, on the other hand, makes you feel more defensive? For me and most consumers I know and study, the answers are easy.

Content Comes in Many Forms

These examples show us how large brands can use content to build relationships and influence customers. But smaller companies have the same capacity as well. Our company's accounting firm employs similar tactics, but in slightly different ways. Their approach shows not only the ability of a small business to do so, but also the many different content vehicles that are available. After all, content is not just long-form writing.

Vestal & Wiler, a small business and personal public accounting service, is the largest independent accounting company in the city of Orlando, Florida. They boast a team of fifty professionals, and our company has utilized their services for a decade. Interestingly enough, they have never "sold" me a single thing. Yet their approach to marketing makes me want to buy plenty.

Vestal & Wiler distributes informative content through a few different vehicles. To begin, they send a monthly e-mail newsletter that is comprised of original articles about trending financial topics. Second, they offer client roundtable events where small groups of clients can share insights and ideas on industry topics such as healthcare reform, mergers, and acquisitions. Third, they send an annual guide to tax law changes that are pertinent to me and our company. In all cases, they seek only to inform—not to sell.

> 80 percent of business decision makers prefer company information in a series of articles instead of an advertisement.
>
> --Custom Content Council

According to Steve Castino, partner, shareholder, and leader of the marketing effort, "We are a marketing-minded sales organization, but we do not seek to interrupt our clients with service offers. Our approach has been to offer helpful advice and information in a structured way and quietly position our firm and brand as the source of expertise. Without overtly asking for it, the revenue has flowed from this approach."

Results like this should not be surprising to us. As consumers, content puts us in the role of the *hunter*, not the *hunted*. According to a survey commissioned by the Custom Content Council, 80 percent of business decision makers prefer company information in a series of articles instead of an advertisement.

Content Marketing Online

As you might imagine, the content marketing approach that started with the likes of John Deere and Jello-O a hundred years ago has risen to a new level by using the advantages of digital tools. Online publishing tools combined with the lack of printing and postage costs have allowed more brands to participate in content marketing activities than ever before.

Since the cost of content distribution is so low (no printing or postage to pay for), brands can disseminate content at will. And the content travels in many forms. Let's take a look at some of the more prevalent forms of online content. As you review them, it may be helpful to have a picture of your audience in mind, as you think about what might have the most appeal to them.

- **Articles.** Writing informative articles about issues affecting your customers' lives or businesses is critical. For example, a florist may write articles about different flower varieties, tips on how to keep your flowers alive longer, or seasonal trends.

- **White Papers.** Similar to an article, a white paper typically takes a position on a particular matter, articulates an argument for something, or presents research findings. White papers typically come in PDF format and look like article reprints that you might order from a magazine. Steelcase, the office furniture manufacturer, houses a number of white papers on its website that reflect the company's research and points of view on workplace efficiency and wellness.
- **Photographs.** People love high-quality pictures, and they are great for posting and sharing. Brands can always find good ways to take advantage of visual opportunities and take pictures of them. A boutique restaurant, for example, can feature photographs of the day's specials or the chef's artistry.
- **Diagrams.** When it comes to explaining things, diagrams are sometimes better than articles. One great example is the Behavior Gap website (www.behaviorgap.com), which uses sketched diagrams to simply and elegantly illustrate complex individual investing principles.
- **Videos.** Video is growing by leaps and bounds online. Informational videos are a great way for people in your company to explain a concept or to convey news. Home Depot's YouTube channel

has thousands of videos featuring tips and how-to segments on how to do things around your home. From tips on painting your home's interior walls to weatherizing your windows, Home Depot has flooded the Internet with free educational material around its brand. The video doesn't always have to be simply instructional, either. Chipotle created a full-blown comedy miniseries called "Farmed and Dangerous" to reinforce its stance on ethical farming through satire.

- **Google+ Hangouts.** Google+ Hangouts has emerged as a fast, low-cost way to hold an online videoconference. The software allows moderators to broadcast the hangout live and to record and post the entire replay on YouTube. While Hangouts are good for general socializing and family gatherings, brands are using the platform for both live and recorded content.

- **Podcasts.** Podcasts come in audio and video form. The podcasting revolution has put pretty much every individual and brand in the position of being a radio or television host on any subject. Users can sign up for podcasts that they like and automatically receive fresh episodes on their mobile phones as the episodes are published. Naturally, radio and television networks such as NBC and NPR are using podcasts as a way to expand their reach, but brands are getting into the mix as well. BMC Software, for instance, uses podcasts to further the company's message on topics such as online courseware development, one of the company's key product areas.

- **Webinars.** Webinars are an excellent way for companies to offer live or recorded presentations on topics that matter to their customers. In an age where an in-person meeting can easily be held online, webinars offer an efficient, affordable way to communicate a structured message. In fact, 61 percent of B2B marketers rated the webinar as a highly effective content marketing tactic, second only to case studies and in-person events (according to a MarketingProfs study). Tools such as GoToMeeting (www.gotomeeting. com) make it easy to hold a webinar, and even record it for repeat broadcast.

> 61 percent of B2B marketers rated the webinar as a highly effective content marketing tactic, second only to case studies and in-person events.
>
> --MarketingProfs

- **Presentation Slides.** Once you have delivered a webinar or in-person presentation, your presentation slides can be published and distributed as well. Perhaps the best-known hub of presentation slides is SlideShare (www.slideshare.net), an online social network (think of SlideShare as the YouTube of presentation slides) that allows you to publish and share your presentations. Law firms, for example, use SlideShare to distribute their slides from speaking engagements and seminars that they give. It is one more way to leverage the work they have done, and to widen the audience of people who are able to view it. Michael Brenner, vice president of marketing at SAP, calls Slideshare the "biggest opportunity in business-to-business (B2B) content marketing."

> Slideshare is the biggest opportunity in business-to-business (B2B) content marketing.
> --Michael Brenner, VP of Marketing, SAP

- **Infographics.** Infographics are an emerging trend online whereby publishers can help users visualize topics. Similar to diagrams, infographics usually illustrate a process, concept, or topic, but they do it in a highly engaging and entertaining way. Coca-Cola has used this approach to illustrate a variety of topics, but a particularly interesting one is their infographic portraying the company's "global commitment to help fight obesity." The colorful graphic helps a consumer visualize some key statistics about Coca-Cola's efforts in a way that is much more inviting than a list of bullets in a document.

- **Other Forms of Content.** There are a great number of other forms of content not listed here. Animated images, motion graphic presentations, and even content widgets such as "this day in history" and collections of facts, figures, and forecasts can all be classified as content. And the list is growing all of the time.

Jane Loves Content

The velocity of leads from content is faster than any other lead we get. Our thinking is that the faster we run this engine, the more leads we will get.

--Rishi Dave, Director of Online Marketing, Dell

Thinking back to our earlier example of Jane, the impatient, Facebook-addicted, Google-searching mother, you can begin to see content as the way to Jane's heart. Jane is looking for answers, information, and a quick guide to help her solve problems. Her tools, devices, and connectivity have conditioned her for it.

When a brand's content is aligned with these search behaviors, the results can be astounding. If you examine the marketing activities at Dell Computer, you will see the fruits of their labor. "The velocity of leads from content is faster than any other lead we get," according to Rishi Dave, Dell's executive director of online marketing. "Our thinking is that the faster we run this engine, the more leads we will get."

Every brand has its own "Jane" that it needs to connect with. In some brand narratives, Jane is single and just started her first job in Manhattan. In others, Jane's kids just started college. Jane is actually *John* in other brand scenarios. Understanding this story—and who Jane really is to your brand—is the first step toward being *Found* by whoever *your* Jane might be.

PART 2:
A FRAMEWORK FOR CONNECTING WITH CUSTOMERS IN THE DIGITAL AGE

> If you always do what you've always done, you'll always get what you've always gotten.
>
> —Mark Twain

Once you accept that the landscape has shifted, you may realize that your organization and its marketing efforts have yet to follow suit. In all fairness, it takes everyone a certain period of time to realize that the shift has happened. Like a slow-boiling pot of water, it is hard to recognize progressive change until the change really materializes and the water is bubbling. Fortunately, though, there are methods to study and steps to take that help you not only adapt to the shift but also profit from it. In this part of the book, we will talk about four separate but interdependent activities that your organization can undertake in order to connect with customers within this landscape. If you imagine your company building a "digital marketing machine," the four activities we prescribe would be interdependent gears. This part of the book will teach you how to develop each gear and to create a truly powerful machine, the output of which is more leads and more revenue.

KNOW THY AUDIENCE

> The aim of marketing is to know and understand the customer so well the product or service fits him and sells itself.
>
> —Peter Drucker

Knowing Your Customer

When our agency begins talking to a new prospect who is interested in working with us, one of the first questions we ask deals with the nature of his or her target market. This is not a particularly original or insightful question, certainly, as any firm worth its salt wants to start with a general understanding of the people who are supposed to be buying the client's product.

Over the years, though, I have often been puzzled by the nature of most of the answers: very few of them reflect a commitment or passion to truly understand the audience. Standard responses are typically vague or broad, like "mostly female, but not all the time," or "pretty much everyone."

> If you try to be all things to all people, you'll end up being nothing to no one.
>
> --Marketing Adage

I believe that these answers are meant to prevent a marketing approach from alienating a particular audience. Understandably, no one wants to implement a marketing tactic that pleases one buyer at the expense of another, but this lack of true engagement, or wrestling with an understanding of a target customer, is troubling from a marketing standpoint. It waters down the impact of marketing efforts because it paints with a very broad brush. But when it comes to content marketing, *knowing your customer* in deep ways—and in the context of your brand—is vital. And in terms of our framework, it is the first of four interdependent activities (or gears) a company must undertake (or deploy) in order to be *Found* by customers.

Exploring Customer Demographics

Once you have made the commitment to invest time into understanding your audience, the first step is to develop an understanding of who they are, from a demographic standpoint. Are your customers male, female, or both? If there is a split, what is the percentage? What age brackets do they typically fall into? Having answers to some of these questions—to the extent that you can answer them—is a good place to start. Some common demographic categories are

- Age
- Gender
- Ethnicity
- Marital status
- Employment status
- Education completed
- Family size
- Income level
- Number of languages spoken
- Occupation type
- Company role
- City/state of residence

Thinking through these areas of demographic data can help you to frame a picture of your customer base. The best way to get good data is to survey your customers. But for those who are comfortable making some assumptions or relying on common knowledge, simply answering the questions on your customers' behalf is a good place to start. And while answering these questions may seem like a chore, going through the exercise can be more instructive than you might think. If you can, have different people in your company complete this exercise separately, and then come together to compare answers. You might be surprised at the different perspectives you see. In the end, you should have a fairly reliable demographic profile of your customer.

Examining Your Demographic Data through a Motivational Lens

Once you have a demographic picture of your audience, you are in a good position to add color to it and bring it to life. A great way to do this is to look at it through the lens of your audience's motivations and concerns. In other words, when it comes to your brand or industry, what do your customers really care about? By cross-referencing the demographic profile with a series of motivation-centric questions, you can begin to understand how content marketing will help you connect with them. Here are some example questions to think about:

- What does a typical day look like for our customers?
- How long is their daily commute, and how do they spend it? Driving? Taking a bus? On a bike?

- What keeps them up at night?
- How much disposable income do our customers have, and how do they spend it?
- What types of technology devices do they prefer, or are they able to afford them?
- What are the generational issues or challenges that this segment faces?
- What does a vacation look like to them?
- What social networks are emerging in importance for this market segment?
- How does this group respond to various forms of advertising?
- What forms of entertainment does this group flock to?
- How much television does this group watch?
- Are there online communities or message boards where this group congregates?
- When it comes to our product, what key messages might be particularly important to this group?
- Apart from our product, what does this group think about our industry?
- What ideals or political issues might be relevant?

Feel free to add other questions that might be relevant to your company. The overall idea is to get you to dig deeper in order to paint a picture of your different market segments.

Naturally, you're not going to have answers to all of these questions. By doing some research on your particular segment and how they interact with online sites and communities, you will quickly find that you can draw various conclusions about different groups, which will ultimately guide your marketing efforts.

Determining Where Your Audience Congregates Online

A key element in this discussion is identifying some places where your audience congregates online. If your idea is limited to the usual suspects of Facebook, Instagram, Google+, Twitter, and LinkedIn, you are likely missing out. The next time you see a SHARE THIS button on a website, take a look at how many sharing avenues there are. Challenge yourself to expand your horizons when it comes to what defines a community or social network, and you might be pleasantly surprised by what you find.

Here are some examples of online communities that are thriving. While all of these won't be appropriate for every audience, they can help to reframe our notion of a social network and challenge us to go deeper:

- **Quora.** Quora (www.quora.com) is an online community where users (primarily business professionals) ask each other questions about particular ideas, strategies, and experiences. You might answer a question asking for cash flow advice, or ask a question related to a legal matter. The idea is to help one another and get to know others in the process.

- **#Longreads.** How can a Twitter hashtag be a community? Just take a look at the #longreads feed (particularly on a weekend), and it may really open your eyes. Readers who have a love of long-form writing are constantly sharing their favorites here.
- **CafeMom.** You can probably guess what this site is about, but CafeMom bills itself as "The Meeting Place for Moms." Users from all around the world can share advice and support on maternal issues, from prenatal difficulties to helping your teenager learn to drive.
- **ModelMayhem.** This is a site for models and photographers to network with one another, share industry best practices, and even find new assignments. The site has grown into a vibrant community where a particular segment is able to build genuine topical exchange.
- **Trip Advisor.** People who love to travel, and who are engaged in the process of doing it better and more cheaply, congregate here. It's a great site for users to research hotel and restaurant tips, as well as write reviews on places you visit. Participating in the site's community has become a hobby for scores of travelers.
- **iVillage.** iVillage was one of the original web destinations for women, and it still thrives as a place where the female audience can learn and share together.

- **Nike+.** The fitness juggernaut Nike created its own community to help athletes connect with one another, share performance tips, and encourage other members with their fitness and nutrition goals. The community also ties in real-time data captured from its mobile apps and wearable devices such as fitness bands, watches, and pedometers.
- **YouTube.** You may think of YouTube merely as a place to watch clips of everything from cute kittens to movie trailers, but it is much more. YouTube is a huge community where passionate hobbyists not only view and comment on videos, but also communicate on current events or life happenings.
- **The Photographer Within.** Have you bought a digital SLR camera and want to really know how to use it? For those who want to take better pictures than those made by a smartphone, figuring out how all of the buttons, dials, settings, and lenses on a "real" camera work can be a bit daunting. The Photographer Within is an online community where thousands of photography enthusiasts from all over the world connect with one another, teach each other techniques, and share feedback on their work.

There are thousands of other examples like this for your brand to be aware of. This list is simply meant to help you expand your horizons when it comes to thinking about where your audience spends time online.

By recommending that you identify your online audiences, I'm not suggesting that you should jump right in and start advertising or spamming to these communities. The nature of content marketing is quite the opposite, leaning toward providing content that does not advertise or sell, but instead informs, persuades, and influences. We will address this topic later in the book when we focus on social media marketing.

The goal is to identify some specific places where your audience hangs out online, so that you can think about different ways to focus your attention on them. However, be careful when you do this. If you paint with a broad brush and limit yourself to Facebook, you'll likely miss the mark. And if you try to satisfy the demands of *all* social networks, you'll likely dilute your efforts. As the famous saying goes, "If you try to be all things to all people, you'll end up being nothing to no one."

Also keep in mind that those who participate in particular communities and social networks change over time. For example, Facebook started as a site exclusively for college students, later picked up the young professionals segment, and eventually went through a phase of growth where those in their fifties and sixties flocked to the site in droves. As you might expect, college students no longer think that Facebook is the coolest place to be!

Developing Audience Profiles

Now that you've done some hard work to learn about the demographics of your audience, what they care about, and where they hang out online, the final step is to create a series of audience profiles based on your findings. We have already introduced you to the idea of audience profiling through our discussion about Jane. If you approach this task with intensity and focus, your likelihood of being *Found* is much greater than if you simply gloss over this issue, as I mentioned in the beginning of this chapter.

The outcome of this exercise should be a series of sketches about the various customer groups that you intend to serve within your audience. Your audience profiles should be detailed, illuminating composites of your data that will drive other elements of your strategy. The result should be a document that is a roster of your customer segments. There is no magic formula for this, but a basic audience profile should contain:

- **Name.** It's helpful to give each profile a fictional name. This "brings the profile to life" in your mind and when you're communicating with your team about that profile.
- **Demographic Snapshot.** Basic, relevant demographic data for that profile.
- **Motivational Overview.** Findings and assumptions about that group's cares and concerns.

- **Online Communities.** Basics about where this group hangs out.

The profiles can be as short or as long as you would like them to be. Emphasize being thorough with the details, without getting too granular. Using a health club as an example, let's look at how a profile might come together.

XYZ Health & Fitness *Audience Profiles*			
Name	**Demographic Snapshot**	**Motivational Overview**	**Online Communities**
Herb	64-year-old male, high net worth, drives a Mercedes	Concerned about cholesterol, high blood pressure, and wants to avoid diabetes	Facebook, LinkedIn, Nike+
Nancy	29-year-old female, shares an apartment with a roommate, commutes on the subway, very little disposable income	Wants to get in great shape for her wedding and maintain her new weight when she gets there	Facebook, Instagram, Twitter
Timmy	16-year-old male, student, lives at home, holds a part-time job	Wants to make his varsity football team, add bulk, and look good with his shirt off	Instagram, Tumblr

Ideally, your profiles should be much more in-depth, but this should give you an idea about how to categorize your audience, how to think about them on deeper levels, and how to ultimately connect with them in more meaningful ways.

YOU NEED A BLOG

> My blog has been the best damn marketing tool
> I've ever had. And it's free.
>
> —Tom Peters

From Skeptic to Believer

Whenever I mention blogging to a business owner as a vital component of a digital marketing strategy, I can almost feel his or her eyes starting to roll. Sadly, blogging has earned a reputation as a self-centered, narcissistic pursuit—the digital equivalent of an adolescent diary.

In the realm of journalism, blogs are often regarded as unverified, low-credibility refuges for wannabe writers. Admittedly, there are many cases where viewpoints like these are validated. But marketers must reconsider these skeptical inner biases if they wish to be *Found*.

Perhaps you are already excited about learning how blogging can make a big impact on a marketing strategy, but if you are still struggling to set aside a dismissive viewpoint, here is one thing to try: substitute the words *publishing platform* or *publishing* anytime you hear the words *blog* or *blogging*, respectively. Although these words aren't entirely interchangeable, it may be helpful in shedding the "teenage diary" notion, if just for a moment. Here are some recent survey data points to consider:

- 57 percent of all marketers gained customers by blogging *(source: HubSpot)*
- 81 percent of US online consumers trust information and advice from blogs. Sixty-one percent of US online consumers have made a purchase based on recommendations from a blog *(source: BlogHer)*
- B2B marketers who use blogs generate 67 percent more leads than those who do not *(source: InsideView)*

These statistics tell us what we anecdotally know to be true: blogging (publishing) is a proven way to help you find new customers by being *Found* by them.

Ultimately, blogging is a way to feed and nurture both your customers (by providing them with valuable information in the spirit of John Deere's turn-of-the-century magazine) and search engines such as Google. Google values content that is helpful to its users, and rewards the publisher with high rankings. Publishing content in this fashion is your vehicle to ensuring that your brand is *Found* in this capacity. Hence, blogging is the second of four gears in the digital marketing machine.

Blogging: It's Not Just for Teenagers and Wannabe Reporters

With few exceptions, I believe that every company needs at least one blog. You can start by thinking of a company blog as a receptacle for content that you create. Along this line of thinking, it's a section of your company website where you can write about new ideas, announcements, and events that are relevant to your firm or industry.

A blog is a place for you to post news that you want your customers and the media to know about. It's also a place for you to answer common questions from your customers and prospects. In short, it's a way to keep your website fresh by having a repository of new and dynamic material that complements those areas of your website—e.g., who we are, what we do, company mission statement—that do not change very often.

Once you have considered a company blog as a repository or receptacle of information, then take your thinking to a level where you liken it to a vehicle or channel—an avenue. Unlike other, more stagnant content pieces, a company blog should be a place where relationships are created and developed. The idea is not only to produce fresh material but also to engage others in it—to share it with others, reinforce your thinking, disagree with it, repurpose it, or simply to bookmark it. Your company blog is a huge opportunity to connect with others. If you haven't already, you should start today.

What Should I Write About?

Deciding what to write about on your blog takes a bit of time. There are very few rules. You aren't constrained by page counts because you aren't printing or physically mailing anything. In short, start by doing and feeling your way along.

Your blog should serve many purposes for your company. It can be an online newsroom for things such as company advisories, event recaps, or news releases. It can be an educational warehouse for things such as product or service updates, case studies where you show your company in action, or commentaries on things you observe. Ultimately, though, the purpose of your blog is to *serve* the needs of your customers, not to *sell* them on something.

How do you do that? Your first step is to review the profiling you have done on your audience. In the previous chapter, we looked at why studying your audience is so important. This is where some of that work begins to pay off.

Each of your customer groups has different interest areas. We saw this in our audience profile of the fictional XYZ Health & Fitness. Herb, for example, is interested in exercise programs that help him to live longer. Nancy wants to lose weight. Timmy, by contrast, wants to gain weight. If you are XYZ Health & Fitness, these are the things you should write about. Write about what *they* care about. To get you started, the following diagram shows some of the common areas of concern that most customers have as they go through life.

THE CLOUD OF CUSTOMER CONCERN

Meeting Basic Needs

Family   Convenience

Wealth & Prosperity   Solving Problems

Saving Time or Money   Health & Fitness

Connecting with Others   Getting Ahead

What Your Customers Care About

Being Prepared   Happiness

Entertainment   Learning New Things

Family Well-Being   Safety & Security

Relaxation   Fulfillment

New Experiences

Independent of your product or service, your customers care about a great many things. Understanding what they truly care about is essential to connecting with them.

Ironically, most of the corporate blogs I see are focused on the company—not the customer. These blogs are not customer-centric but "marketing director-centric." Perhaps showing a weakness in audience understanding or perhaps just a lack of planning, most company blogs are poorly executed. They might post three or four times a year, and they often display a lack of topic structure or organization. Posts read like advertisements ("Here at Johnson & Associates, we are top-notch at what we do") or are simply corporate pats on the back (e.g., we won an award, we celebrated our fifth anniversary). None of these things is inherently bad; they're just not things that your customers *care* about. The challenge is to be substantive and relevant, not self-interested and trivial. The following table shows some examples of each:

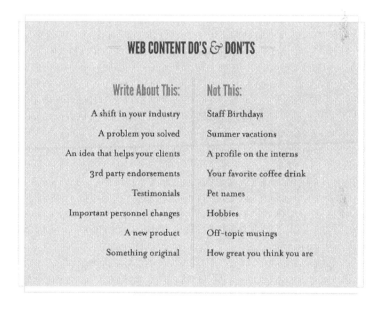

WEB CONTENT DO'S & DON'TS	
Write About This:	**Not This:**
A shift in your industry	Staff Birthdays
A problem you solved	Summer vacations
An idea that helps your clients	A profile on the interns
3rd party endorsements	Your favorite coffee drink
Testimonials	Pet names
Important personnel changes	Hobbies
A new product	Off-topic musings
Something original	How great you think you are

This list of things to write about or avoid can help you stay focused on what *your customers* truly care about, as opposed to the things that *you* might care about.

In the opening chapter of this book we introduced Jane, a fictional character who is on the go, self-interested, and has little time on her hands. Jane does not care about your latest award or what you say about yourself. She cares about solving her own problems, improving her life, and moving on. The challenge of publishing good content is to satisfy Jane *while* promoting your product. A good blog focuses on posts that discuss what you do *and* what your customers care about, as portrayed in the diagram below.

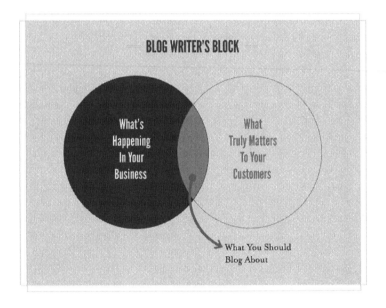

Finding the overlap between *what's happening in your business* and *what your customers care about* should guide what you write about on your blog.

Blogging & Parachute Moments

The Holy Grail in corporate blogging is to write to your customers' parachute moments—those times when their needs are particularly elevated—in the context of your product. When most of us are in parachute moments, we use Google to help us. According to a study by the Pew Research Center, the Internet is the most turned-to source for people when it comes to solving their problems. Fifty-eight percent of respondents indicated that when they encounter a common problem, they turn to the Internet. Only 45 percent said they sought out friends and family members, and 13 percent went to the public library.

> Fifty-eight percent of survey respondents indicated that when they encounter a common problem, they turn to the Internet.
>
> --Pew Research Center

Ideally you want your customers to find you when they go looking for answers. This is precisely why the term inbound marketing is used interchangeably with content marketing. The content draws the customers *inward*. We will talk more about search marketing and search engine optimization (SEO) in a later chapter, but for the time being, it is helpful to set the stage in this way: the content you publish on your blog should solve your customers' problems—not tout your latest industry award.

Let's look at a practical example of this. I was recently asked by a university to conduct a webinar for some companies that the university was incubating. I don't conduct webinars frequently, so I had a couple of questions about the best practices of duration, platform, and other areas. But one of the most pressing questions on my mind was *when* to conduct the webinar. I was curious about the best day of the week, and what time of the day, to schedule it. Like the respondents in the Pew Research Center study, I Googled my question.

I typed, "What is the best time to schedule a webinar?" into Google. There, on the first page of search results, was a blog post from AccuConference, a software company that helps people like me conduct webinars.

When I clicked on the link, I was taken to a well-constructed page that contained the company's expert opinion on what days and times tend to work best for businesspeople to attend webinars. And even though the blog post was not a sales pitch, I was introduced to their product in my time of need—my parachute moment. What this company had done, presumably, was simply to anticipate my question, and answer it.

Question Everything

One great takeaway from this example is the fact that users (like me) ask Google their questions. Most instances on Google are referred to as *queries*—another word for questions. We ask, and they answer.

In essence, search engines such as Google, Yahoo, and Bing are glorified answer machines. Yahoo even has its own subsite called Yahoo Answers, where users post questions and other members answer them. (This is another example of a social network or community, by the way.)

When it comes to your blog, a great way to meet your users' needs is to anticipate their questions and write the answers in advance. If Jane wants to know about upcoming local summer camps for her kids, she might type a question like this into the Google search bar: "What are the best summer camps in Topeka?" If you feel strongly that this is the type of question your customer would ask, then you should have a blog post entitled, "What are the best summer camps in Topeka?" or something similar. In this context, remember that content marketing is about informing and influencing—not advertising or selling.

A great way to focus on generating these questions is to get your team together and talk about what questions are commonly asked by your customers in day-to-day business dealings. As a digital marketing agency, we get questions all the time that help us frame our thinking.

Some of the more common questions we receive in both business development and client service conversations are:

- How do you get to the top of the rankings on Google?
- Once we start a Facebook page for our company, what should we put on it?
- How do I measure the ROI of my social media spending?

All these questions can be turned into specific blog posts that simply regurgitate the answers we commonly give them. It bears repeating that our answers should be written to objectively inform and educate—not to sell or advertise.

I thought about this recently when I was struggling to remove some very stubborn adhesive from a section of hardwood flooring using warm soapy water and a coarse sponge. I wasn't making much progress and my frustration turned into a parachute moment. When I entered "how do I remove adhesive from hardwood floors?" into Google, I was presented with videos, blog posts, and other diagrams from brands like Home Depot, Behr, and others anxious to sell me products and supplies to get the job done. This ultimately led me to a purchase. All brands can leverage this effect simply by anticipating these questions and answering them with published content.

We will talk in more detail about the mechanics of search marketing later in the book, but for the time being, remember that search engines are really built upon questions. Your blog should be prepared to answer them. As you begin to develop a format for your audience profiles that makes sense to you, consider adding a column for them within your documentation.

Develop an Editorial Calendar

Thinking about creating all of this content can seem pretty overwhelming at first, but it can be manageable with solid planning, thoughtful division of labor, and a recognition that this is an investment in the future of your company—not simply another company chore. In order to create a smooth process for a steady flow of relevant posts, a forward-looking plan of attack can really help. Magazines and newspapers call this an "editorial calendar" and, as a publisher, you should have one for your blog.

An editorial calendar can take many forms, but the basic idea is to create a schedule within a simple chart that addresses who will be writing posts, what the topics will be, when they will be written, who will edit or proof them, etc. Although your editorial calendar may be simple or complex, the basic parameters you may wish to consider are as follows:

- Submission Deadline
- Publication Date
- Author
- Editor/Approver

- Editorial Topic Area
- Blog Post Title
- Imagery
- Word Count
- Focus Keyword(s)
- Audience Profile(s) to be Targeted

Most companies have multiple blog authors, which can really help with the ongoing content creation. Dividing the labor can be crucial to the success of the effort so that one person does not get overwhelmed. Working together as a group to brainstorm blog topics in advance can also help to keep all team members on the same page with topics. Deciding topics in advance can also help with the all-too-common refrain of "I have no idea what to write about."

Using our example of XYZ Health & Fitness, a sample editorial calendar segment may look like the following:

XYZ Health & Fitness Blog Editorial Calendar		
Submission Date	11/2/14	11/15/14
Publication Date	11/7/14	11/28/14
Author	Tom	Suzy
Editor/Approver	Roger	Roger
Editorial Topic Area	Weight Training	Nutrition
Blog Post Title	How Do I Add Muscle Bulk to My Upper Body?	Ten Tips for Fighting Evening Cravings
Imagery	Barbells, Bench	Photo of Smoothie
Word Count	450	450
Focus Keyword(s)	Add muscle, upper body	Cravings, hunger
Audience Profile(s) to Be Targeted	Timmy	Nancy

You can certainly expand upon this format quite dramatically, but having some basic guidance like the parameters above can go a long way toward ensuring a return on the resources you are investing in this endeavor. In absence of a content plan of some sort, you will likely find that blog posts are sporadic, off-topic, and lacking in real substance.

Blog Post Fundamentals: A Checklist

As you think about turning multiple people loose to create blog content according to a preset schedule, you should also establish some ground rules to ensure that the content is well-received by your audience and search engines alike. While there are no hard and fast rules as to what you should post on your blog—sometimes you may just share a single image, for example—it is a good idea to establish some uniform guidelines for your blog posts. Uniformity can be helpful, and guidelines can help your authors get started. Some of the more common checklist items are as follows:

Company Blog Post Checklist

- Word count is over 300
- Post is well-structured, with appropriate introduction and conclusion
- Focus Keyword is present in title, URL, and body copy multiple times
- Spelling and grammar have been checked and corrected

- Post features one or two interesting images that are used with permission or under proper licensing
- Images include proper tags and captions
- The post links to existing blog posts on the blog and other relevant external sources
- Content is genuinely useful to others and likely to be shared by the target audience
- The post has been categorized and tagged according to the conventions of the company's chosen blogging platform
- All content is original or includes proper citations and links to third-party content
- Content focuses on the needs of the audience—not the company—and does not advertise or sell
- Topics and statements include references to facts, figures, and other empirical data

Like the editorial calendar, having uniform guidelines in place helps you to manage the structure, flow, and quality of the content in your blog. Remember that there are no universal "rules" per se, but adopting and instituting some general best practices will help you start on the right foot and stay on track as you move forward.

Blogging Keys to Remember

Now that you are well on your way to generating meaningful, relevant content in your blog, here are some common ideas to remember and think about as you go forward:

- **Results Take Time.** As with any worthwhile pursuit, success doesn't happen overnight. It takes six, nine, or twelve months to start seeing real momentum develop. Unfortunately, many company blogging efforts are abandoned after only a month or two when results don't immediately pour in. Blogger Huyen Truong described his experience with an Australian car company with which he was consulting. After twelve months of regularly creating and posting content on their blog, the company was able to increase monthly visits to the site from 400 to 8,600—multiplying traffic *twenty-one times* over. If you employ a long-term view and some patience, the effort will eventually pay off. Let the following diagram serve as a visual reminder that patience pays, and that you should not abandon the process if you don't see immediate results:

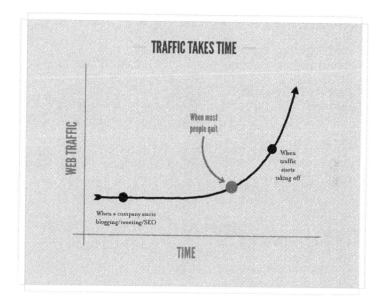

When people start blogging, many of them quit after only a few months because they don't see results quickly enough. Building traffic through blogging takes time. *(Adapted from Moz)*

- **Blogging Success Requires Volume.** If you want to see a true business impact from your blog, remember that you have to create and fill your blogging pipeline with a great deal of content. A blog post or two every six weeks won't cut it. According to a recent HubSpot survey, businesses that blog twenty times per month get five times more traffic than those that blog fewer than four times per month. That statistic heavily reinforces the notion that churning out a high volume of content is critical to success.

- **Your Blog Should Be Inside Your Company Website.** It may seem like a given, but it is all too common for businesses to create blogs and host them on other domains or with third-party blogging services such as WordPress or Blogger. These are wonderful free platforms, but housing all of your blog content on *their* website (www.blogger.com/xyzhealth) instead of your own (www.xyzhealth.com/blog) gives all of the search engine "credit" to their site. Accomplished blogger Geraldine DeRuiter likens this to "doing a bunch of repairs and upgrades to a rental car"—a point she made after reflecting on important lessons learned after writing a thousand blog posts and monitoring their progress. Keep in mind that it's certainly a best practice to use a blogging platform (we use WordPress the most), but be sure it is installed on *your* site, not on someone else's.
- **Don't Forget the Images.** It can be easy to get too focused on the writing and forget the imagery. While the written content is certainly important, we can't forget the importance of imagery. As a society, we're becoming more drawn to and influenced by imagery over the written word.

Blog posts with relevant photos get 94 percent more views than articles without images.

--Skyword

So it's important to include those in your blog posts because they attract users to the textual content. As you browse news sites and blogs, notice that posts presented in menus and feeds are often accompanied by images. That's no accident, and research confirms the importance of including imagery. According to software maker Skyword, blog posts with relevant photos get 94 percent more views than articles without images.

- **Blogging Is a Relationship Framework.** In your quest to create a blog and develop a pipeline of content, remember that blogging is not just a digital receptacle of content—it's a vehicle to connect with others. Take the time to connect with other bloggers, share links, comment on each other's posts, and even post on each other's sites. These connections can really help you in developing your audience and building relationships.

Armed with these additional keys, you'll be well on your way to creating a successful blogging program within your company. Think of yourself as a brand publisher, craft a plan, and employ some patience. And if you look at the program as a long-term investment, you'll be well on your way to finding true momentum. From there, your cumulative efforts will begin to build, like a snowball rolling down a hill.

SEARCH MARKETING FOR THE REST OF US

> Great things are done by a series of small things brought together.
>
> —Vincent Van Gogh

The View from Thirty Thousand Feet

This book is not a how-to guide for tacticians, coders, and designers to learn the latest and greatest tactics about search engine optimization (SEO). There are plenty of books on the market that meet this need. In addition, the SEO world changes too quickly and too dramatically for me to include SEO tactics in this book. By the time the book came off the printing press, the information would already be outdated.

That said, search marketing fundamentals are too important for marketers *not* to be aware of. I believe that almost every executive needs to be aware of the basic fundamentals of SEO in order to be competitive in the "always on" world. Everyone in an organization needs to be thinking about how the search-dependent consumer of today is impacted by his or her role—and how each team member can contribute to the company's SEO success. Search engine marketing is the third gear in the digital marketing machine.

This chapter focuses on the general principles that are important for you to know as a marketer and the person who oversees your company's marketing efforts. I'll help you develop a "framework" for understanding how search engines work, so you can manage the process from thirty thousand feet. This process includes both the practice of SEO and those SEO experts who can help you execute.

Search Engines: A Framework for Understanding

A marketer who truly wants to succeed in the "always on" world that Jane lives in must develop a general knowledge of how search engines work. Understanding search engine behavior is like understanding a major city that you visit for the first time: it's impossible to grasp it completely in a day or a week. You have to establish a bird's-eye view, explore different areas one at a time, and accept that you'll never see everything. In addition, you have to remember that things are changing and moving all the time, and that you will have different opinions about various areas and pursuits.

I realized this the first time I visited Paris, France. For months I prepared for my trip with family and friends by studying maps, reading books, listening to podcasts, and watching cable TV programs. I was determined to conquer all twenty *arrondissements* (districts) of the "City of Light" in ten days flat.

When I first arrived, however, it was clear that one could never do it all—not even in *fifty* trips! There were too many districts, too much depth and history in every street, and more museums than you could ever hope to count. What's more, everything was changing right before our eyes, all the time.

Like an expansive city, SEO also has its vastness, constant change, mystery, and countless moving parts. As a good tour guide might recommend, my advice would be to start understanding SEO from a "big picture" standpoint, then start to explore. Over time, you will begin to feel comfortable and learn your way around.

Over the course of the last two decades I have developed and refined a methodology to help marketing executives understand the vast municipality that is SEO. I have used this methodology in speeches, webinars, writing, and even as subject matter in expert witness testimony. And though the mechanics of search engines change all the time, I have found that this framework has stood the test of time in terms of providing executives with a working knowledge of the landscape. The major steps in the cycle are described below:

- **Keyword Research.** Any meaningful approach to succeeding with search marketing for your business has to begin with an intensive look at what keywords your customers are using as they look for things online during the moments they need your service—their "parachute moments." There are free tools from Google and Bing that help you do this research, as well as paid services such as Wordtracker that can help you look at deeper data. They can help you understand how many times a particular term is searched, and to identify unexpected word combinations that you hadn't thought of. The bottom line is that your team has to do some homework on what words are being used, and not rely on gut instinct alone. Ultimately it is this data that should inform the "focus keywords" segment of your editorial calendar.

- **Website Optimization.** Sometimes called "onsite optimization," website optimization is the process of ensuring that your website and its individual pages are technically and composition-ally structured in a manner to be well received by search engines. Search engines evaluate your site's domain, website construct, and individual web pages for hundreds of factors. Then the search engines make an objective determination about when to present your pages to users with respect to their keyword searches. This is why it is important in your blog posts, for example, to be sure to include target keywords in prominent places within your content. This is one of the factors that search engines evaluate when they look at your blog posts.

- **Off-Site Optimization.** In addition to evaluating a number of parameters within the confines of your website and blog, search engines make determinations about the way your site is regarded by other sites and users. This is a primary factor that propelled Google into an eight-hundred-pound gorilla that trounced its competitors in the search engine business. Google's algorithm was built by counting how many links a site had coming to it from others, and regarding those links as "votes." The more links a site had coming to it, the more relevant the site was presumed to be. If a website about fixing your broken iPhone had hundreds of other pages linking to it, it stood a much better chance of being highly ranked than sites that had no links at all. Now, years later, experts theorize that Google monitors how many pages receive shares, likes, and Tweets—characterized as "social signals"—from sites such as Google+, Twitter, and Facebook to determine how relevant a page is.

- **Campaign Implementation.** Once you have developed on-site and off-site optimization strategies, your next step is to implement a series of the chosen tactics. A two-to-four-month strategy of implementation is a good target in terms of creating content, building links, and engaging your social audience. While performing these tasks on an almost indefinite basis is advisable, segmenting the activities into a finite stretch (or campaign) is also a good path to take. Once you have completed a period of doing so, then it's time to take stock of the results.

- **Performance Reporting & Analysis.** Following the implementation of any campaign to generate search activity, the final step in this (continual) cycle is to measure the effects of your efforts. There are many ways to do this, but the best is to rely on web analytics software tools such as Google Analytics, a free tool offered by Google that provides you with all sorts of metrics. Web analytics software can help you measure site traffic fluctuations, which search engines are driving traffic to your site, and what pages are drawing the most activity. Reviewing these results with your team will help you understand which areas of your efforts are working better than others. Following that process, you will be in a position to resume the cycle by starting at the Keyword Analysis phase again and repeating the steps.

The steps described above are best understood in the form of a cyclical model—a continual process that can serve as an ongoing initiative within a company or marketing team. We've developed this model over the years and call it the Search Engine Success Methodology. While many of the skills required to complete these steps can be learned over time by individual team members, specialists and consultants can also help with different aspects as well. From a management perspective, though, the key is to understand the general idea of the process and to be sure it is implemented by the proper tacticians. The following diagram shows the steps of the cycle, in order:

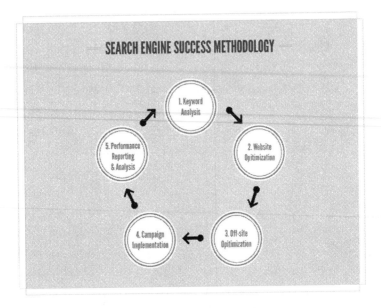

The cycle diagram above shows the various steps in
the Search Engine Success Methodology.

SEO and Parachute Moments

Now that you have a view of the search engine process
from thirty thousand feet, let's look at how and why it
matters to your company and your marketing efforts.
Returning to our image of Jane, it is plain to see that
her dependence on Google for answers to her questions
is *our* marketing opportunity to answer the bell. We just
have to know how to anticipate her parachute moments
and respond.

The hard part is in knowing what those moments are, and being creative about how to integrate them into your search engine optimization strategy. Revisiting our fitness center example, the knee-jerk reaction for most marketers is simply to focus on terms that mirror the company's services—"fitness center" or "personal trainer"—and be done with it. But those terms are often highly competitive, and it's an uphill battle to gain rankings for them. And while I don't think the SEO strategy should ignore these terms, the overall approach should go deeper.

A search marketing strategy should focus deeply on the audience personas we developed as part of our previous chapter about understanding your audience. Building upon our audience profile document, you can add a column for "Likely Search Phrases" (see table below), which reflects anticipated searches:

XYZ Health & Fitness *Audience Profiles*				
Name	**Demographic Snapshot**	**Motivational Overview**	**Online Communities**	**Likely Search Phrases**
Herb	64-year-old, male, high net worth, drives a Mercedes	Concerned about cholesterol, high blood pressure, and wants to avoid diabetes	Facebook, LinkedIn, Nike+	How does exercise affect cholesterol levels? How do I lower my LDL levels?
Nancy	29-year-old, female, shares an apartment with a roommate, commutes on the subway, very little disposable income	Wants to get in great shape for her wedding and maintain her new weight when she gets there	Facebook, Instagram, Twitter	What is the best way to lose weight? What exercises help to tone my arms?
Timmy	16-year-old, male, student, lives at home, holds a part-time job	Wants to make his varsity football team, add bulk, and look good with his shirt off	Instagram, Tumblr	How many calories per day should I eat? How do I add bulk to my chest?

Building search profiles can supplement your keyword research, which should drive both your search marketing efforts and your overall content strategy.

SEO: The Executive's Role

As a marketer or manager, your job is not to memorize the details of this framework or even to understand all of the mechanics and nuances of the individual steps. But executives should know that there are multiple steps to be taken if you want to be *Found* when customers ask Google a question during their parachute moments. Let me explain why.

Over the years I have worked with many executives who desperately want to generate traffic from search engines, but they like to imagine that taking only one of the steps (without pondering the others) will ultimately lead to success. When I talk to them about search marketing, they claim they are "already doing all of that." What they typically mean is that they are doing one or two things but are dismissing the rest. Here are examples of this form of SEO success "denial":

- **The Aimless Blogger.** Some companies update their blogs from time to time, but they never stop to perform keyword research to determine what words or phrases their customers might be using. Google may see these sites, but unfortunately it's for the wrong reasons.

- **The Keyword Stuffer.** Other marketers may have a good grip on the keywords their prospects search for, but their sites have no flow of content to speak of. As a result, the sites look like stagnant, algae-covered ponds to Google.

- **The Remote Island.** Some firms update their blogs with the right keywords, but there is no effort to build links or engage the social media world with the content. As a result, the activity on the site is like a tropical island in the middle of the ocean: pretty to look at, but with no connection to the outside world.

There are other examples that I could use, but hopefully you can see the logic behind taking a comprehensive approach to search marketing, as opposed to an isolated, scattered one. Marketers must understand the bigger picture about driving search engine results, commit to the steps, and take a coordinated approach—not a myopic one.

The other main job for executives is to see SEO as a long-term investment, not as a quick-hitting tactic. I encourage marketers to look at SEO as a *marathon*, not a quick walk around the block. It takes planning, commitment, effort, and patience to get there. Once you begin to gain traction, however, the rewards are high, and so is the satisfaction. What's more, the success that begins to materialize from your *investment* can grow exponentially. At that point you are in a strong position to start realizing short-term benefits almost on demand.

SEO Resources for Executives

Another, more foundational, role for executives is to commit to some level of ongoing education in the area of search marketing. Fortunately, there is a ton of information freely available online about SEO. *Unfortunately,* it can all be pretty overwhelming. To save you a little trouble and research, here are a handful of resources for you to visit and stay abreast of—either through web browser bookmarks or through a social media site such as Twitter or Facebook:

- *How Search Works* (Google): A simple, interactive site that shows you the practicalities of how search works. It is interesting, fun, and very helpful. www.google.com/intl/en_us/insidesearch/howsearchworks/thestory
- *The Periodic Table of SEO Success Factors* (Search Engine Land): This visual guide is a straightforward view of the different factors that play into search success. The table segments on-site factors from off-site factors in a simple way. www.searchengineland.com/seotable
- *Search Ranking Factors Survey* (Moz): This site publishes a regular (every other year) survey of industry experts to gauge what tactics are driving search results and what trends are emerging. This survey should be required reading for executives, although it's a bit technical. www.moz.com/seo-industry-survey
- *Search Engine Land*: This site is a deep reservoir of content on SEO tactics and industry trends. Scanning this site is a bit like drinking from a fire hose, but its topics and subject matter are

almost always relevant. www.searchengineland.
com

- *Moz Blog*: Moz is a leading software company in
  the SEO sector, and their team members are
  great about sharing insights and news about how
  they see search marketing evolving. Keep an eye
  out for their "Whiteboard Friday" posts, where
  they post brief instructional videos on different
  SEO topics. www.moz.com/blog

I am sure that you will find many other resources
that are helpful to you, but these are a few starter links.
Committing to some level of ongoing education in the
SEO space is every executive's job. Again, I certainly
do not believe that marketers should eat, breathe, and
sleep SEO, but they should be familiar with the landscape and be sure that someone on their team has SEO
as a primary function within his or her role. If you accept that your customers (like Jane) are using Google to
find answers to everyday questions, you will want to be
sure that your company's efforts in this area are sound.

SOCIAL MEDIA MARKETING

> Advertising is the price you pay for unremarkable thinking.
>
> —Jeff Bezos

The Social Media Tidal Wave

I can't overstate the impact that online social networks such as Facebook and Twitter have had on our lives, our culture, and commerce. And it's hard to believe that, for as much change as they have introduced, they have only been around for a few years. The change has been significant, unannounced, and quick—a tidal wave.

> 91 percent of online adults use social media regularly.
>
> --Experian

Although much change has been introduced, and the signs of its arrival are so apparent, many businesses are just standing around watching—and not responding. Many marketers are still in denial, wishing that things hadn't changed. But they have.

The statistics about the arrival and impact of social media aren't hard to find. According to Experian, 91 percent of online adults use social media regularly. Much of this usage happens on mobile devices. According to Lightspeed Research, 73 percent of smartphone owners access social networks through mobile apps at least once per day.

The volume of users on these social networks is staggering, according to *Social Media Today*. Facebook boasts over one billion users. Twitter and Google+ both report over five hundred million users each. LinkedIn is a collection of 238 million business users. The list goes on and on—numbers that are too big to count.

> 70 percent of active online adult social networkers shop online.
>
> --Nielsen

But what's transpiring on these networks is not just time wasting and game playing, as many social networking naysayers claim. For starters, it's a spending crowd. According to Nielsen, 70 percent of active online adult social networkers shop online. That's 12 percent more than the Internet user who doesn't use social networking. Social networkers also guide each other's purchase behavior. According to SproutSocial, 74 percent of consumers rely on social networks to guide purchasing decisions. And a staggering 81 percent of participants in a Forbes study indicated that social media posts directly influenced their purchase decisions.

These statistics tell the story of social networking's impact on business. Real transactions are happening there. And if the statistics aren't enough to tell the story, take a look at what really happens on social networks. If you have spent any time on Facebook, for example, you will see people ask each other questions about the money they intend to spend. *Anyone know of a reliable handyman? Can someone recommend a yoga studio that's inviting for beginners? Where should I eat while I'm in Chicago? Can someone recommend an inexpensive laptop I can buy for my mom?* These are all questions I saw on Facebook over the course of just a few days. And while I will concede that there is a ton of time wasting that occurs, this activity is proof that real commerce happens there.

> 74 percent of consumers rely on social networks to guide purchasing decisions.
>
> --SproutSocial

If you want to be *Found*, you have to be in the arena where customers are looking to do business—online so-cial networks. Among other things, social networks are the railroad tracks upon which your content travels. In the words of Jonathan Perelman, president of Buzzfeed, "Content is king but distribution is queen and she wears the pants." The tidal wave has arrived, and the opportunity to harness its power is too great to ignore.

Wading into the Water

> 81 percent of survey participants indicated that so-cial media posts directly influenced their purchase decisions.
>
> --Forbes

If you make the decision that joining the ranks of the social media world is right for your company (or revisiting it if you've had a false start), there are a number of initial steps to take or revisit. There are many different ways to think about this process, but the prescribed best practice is to develop a strategic plan for how you would like to do so.

There is no "right way" to develop a social media plan. Depending upon the size of your company, you might start with a cocktail napkin or single sheet of paper. In larger companies, it might be a fifty-page document that is blessed by numerous management layers. In general, though, your plan should lay out a course for engaging with others in social networks by addressing a few different core areas:

- **Goals & Objectives We Will Pursue.** Almost any planning process should begin by exploring the expected outcomes of the plan itself. This endeavor will involve an investment of resources by the company, so it is important to gauge its return. Common goal areas of a social media plan include web traffic growth, lead generation, sales, referrals, and overall exposure.

- **Social Networks We Will Join.** There are hundreds of social networks and communities from which to choose, so it is best to start small with just a few, and then expand as you see fit. How do you decide which ones to join? Simply consult your audience profiling and compare it to research about the social networks available to you. We will explore the specifics of the social networks later in this chapter.

- **Content We Will Share.** Once you decide what social networks you will get involved with, you have to think about what sort of content will be shared within them. The majority of the content will be from your blog, but deciding how it will be updated, and how the content will vary between platforms, is important. For example, your posts on Facebook may be more story-oriented, while those on Instagram will be image-heavy.

- **Who Will Be Involved.** The next area of focus in the plan is a rundown of what company personnel will be involved. A description of the roles and responsibilities of the various team members (both internal and external) is critical to the success of the effort.

- **Policies We Will Adopt and Adhere To.** Another aspect of the plan is to adopt and implement a social media policy within the organization. Clear policy language will help personnel decide how to engage with users, how to respond to complaints, and what the guidelines are for the propriety of content.

- **How We Will Measure Our Success.** Because the goals a social media plan includes are so important, measuring them from time to time is critical as well. Your social media plan should speak to the various metrics you will track, how often you will update them, and how you will circulate them. It is usually best to create a simple scorecard or social marketing dashboard to give stakeholders a clear, consistent view of progress and success.

- **How We Will Adjust.** German military strategist Helmuth von Moltke famously said that "no battle plan survives contact with the enemy." In other words, be prepared to adjust your plans based upon what transpires, both positive and negative. Revisit your plans periodically, and adjust them based upon how the performance unfolds.

If you don't already have a social media plan, the areas described above can help you get started with creating one. While no two social media plans will look alike, a useful one will include some of these core components.

Pick a Network, Any Network

> Content is king but distribution is queen and she wears the pants.
>
> --Jonathan Perelman, President, Buzzfeed

We have already noted that there are many social networks through which marketers can engage with customers. Because most companies can only manage a small number of them, it is usually a good idea to start with some of the larger, more established networks. Each network has its advantages and nuances. To help you get started, we will look at some of the larger social networks.

- **Facebook.** Facebook is the largest, most accessible social network. Many users look for a company's Facebook page before they look for the company website. Facebook's audience cuts across all demographics, with more recent growth coming from older generations. It's important to create a business presence on Facebook by establishing a company page, called "Pages" within the Facebook platform. Once you've established your company page, you can invite people to join, share photos and stories from your blog, and even buy ads to increase your audience or promote a particular post. Facebook may not be for every company, but it pretty much is. If your company is not alive and kicking on Facebook, it really ought to be.

- **Google+.** Google+ (Google Plus) launched in 2011 as an answer to Facebook and quickly rose to prominence due to the strength of Google as a whole. Google+ feels similar to Facebook, but it skews to a younger audience (average age of twenty-eight vs. Facebook's thirty-eight), is generally perceived to be more popular with males, and attracts more of a tech-heavy audience. Google+

is very important to all companies, though, because of its observed impact on search results. It is generally recognized that content that is shared and promoted in this social network will be more heavily rewarded by Google in search rankings. So be sure to create a brand page for your company on Google+, and follow the authorship verification processes there. According to Eric Schmidt, Google's executive chairman, "Information tied to verified online profiles will be ranked higher than content without such verification...the true cost of remaining anonymous, then, might be irrelevance." This is a prime example of how social media engagement impacts search rankings.

Twitter. Twitter is also an important social network. On Twitter, users share short posts that are limited to 140 characters each. It is a huge area of activity for consumers who like to share news, interact with celebrities, and comment on current events or entertainment broadcasts.

> Eighty percent of leads now start with a referral. Those referrals often start on Twitter.
>
> --Sheryl Pattek, Forrester Research

MIT faculty member Deb Roy referred to Twitter as the "social soundtrack" of television in his observation of the global conversation that transpires between users on Twitter around television shows or live broadcasts. This "conversation" represents an opportunity for a brand to engage. What's more, Twitter helps business to business (B2B) marketers *sell*. According to Forrester Research's Sheryl Pattek, "eighty percent of leads now start with a referral. Those referrals often start on Twitter."

- **LinkedIn.** LinkedIn is the place for professionals to congregate and communicate. This social network is a must if your company sells to, or recruits, professionals. It also has a very powerful ad network where companies can pay for exposure to different segments of professionals. It is a safe assumption that LinkedIn is the most powerful B2B social networking platform.

- **Instagram.** Instagram came out of nowhere and is now owned by (yet operates independently of) Facebook, on a massive scale. Its currency is photography, and individuals and brands share their images and interact with one another there. Consumer marketers have used this network to engage users, build brands, and extend their reach using photos and videos.

- **Pinterest.** Similar to Instagram, Pinterest is a social networking platform that thrives on imagery. This audience is known to be predominantly female (84 percent, according to Nielsen) and its members interact with one another by posting and sharing images on boards that cater to particular interests. Users "pin" images they like onto "pinboards" they create. Many users claim that they use Pinterest to gather inspiration for personal and professional projects they are working on.

- **FourSquare.** FourSquare is a social network where people primarily share information on their location by "checking in" to destinations (stores, restaurants, etc.). Users can keep tabs on each other, meet up, or share comments on the locations that come up in their day-to-day interactions.

- **Spotify.** Spotify is an online music service, integrated with Facebook, where users can follow each other's musical tastes and activities. I can follow the playlists of my friends and find out what artists and songs they like, as well as discover emerging artists.

- **Tumblr.** Similar to Twitter, Tumblr is a micro-blogging platform without the 140-character limitation. Users can post and share both long-form content as well as brief updates or images. A popular form of content on this network is animated imagery of either a trending joke, meme, or current event. Tumblr's demographics skew to a younger audience segment, but it happens to be a very engaged group that is quite valuable to marketers. Brands can successfully enter this realm with a healthy mix of humor, wit, and sarcasm.

- **Yelp.** Yelp is another social network that thrives primarily on the exchange of location-based information. The twist, though, is that Yelp encourages users to rate and review the restaurants, stores, and other destinations they visit. In aggregate, stores can earn positive or negative user ratings based upon the customers' experiences. If you are providing a great product or service at a retail destination, Yelp can really help you get the word out.

E-mail Marketing. You may be surprised to see this tactic listed within a series of social media tools, but it is useful to look at it in this context.

> The inbox is the most important social network of all.
>
> --Chris Brogan, Publisher, *Owner* Magazine

According to Chris Brogan, publisher of *Owner* Magazine and recognized marketing expert, the "inbox is the most important social network of all." The data is not at odds with his assessment. A recent McKinsey & Company study concluded that e-mail is nearly forty times more effective than Twitter or Facebook when it comes to acquiring customers.

- **The Next Big Thing.** This is only a small sampling of the social networks that a brand can use to interact online with customers. Keep in mind that there are many more to learn about and discover. Also, don't forget that new social networking sites are springing up constantly. You never know which one might be the "next big thing," and quickly go from obscurity to relevance.

> Information tied to verified online profiles will be ranked higher than content without such verification...the true cost of remaining anonymous, then, might be irrelevance.
>
> --Eric Schmidt, Executive Chairman, Google

These networks are certainly ones that you should consider as you go about planning your path to taking advantage of the social media tidal wave. The best way to learn about them is to join networks that you think are pertinent to you, talk to other users about how they use them, and engage with other users you find there. Most social networks are very welcoming to newcomers.

Social Media Philosophy 101

> No battle plan survives contact with the enemy.
>
> --Helmuth von Moltke

With all of these social networking tools available, the massive number of people on these platforms, and the fact that most of them are free to join, there is an overwhelming temptation for marketers to use the tools as one big advertising billboard. In reality, though, the real winners on social networking platforms are the ones who approach it with a much different philosophy: as a platform to build real relationships based upon sharing, community, and inspiration—not selling. And while sales certainly can come out of the process as a natural outgrowth, companies must engage in social networking with a truly authentic, user-centric approach. While every brand will have its own philosophy on how this works for them, here are some of the key factors that I have observed:

- **Listen.** Social networking relationships thrive when the communication is two-way. So be sure to listen to those who communicate with you, even if they complain. Don't just look at it as a platform for your brand to speak.
- **Share Interesting Content.** This harkens back to earlier thoughts on blogging. Be sure to create

and/or share unique content that truly helps users solve their problems. Your users will tell you how valuable it is to them by how often they like, share, retweet, or repin it.

- **Be Social.** The nature of these platforms is to be warm, inviting, and friendly in the same way you would at a barbecue. Most consumers use social networks as a way to have fun, learn, or take a break. Your brand has the opportunity to be a positive part of that experience—assuming your approach is one that truly is social.

- **Help Others.** We all know that you reap what you sow. When you sow seeds of courtesy or favors, you are likely to see them blossom for you down the road in the form of returns. As with life, you shouldn't do a favor and keep score of who returns it. Just know that a spirit of doing for and giving to others goes along with a degree of success in your efforts.

- **Be Consistent and Active.** For brands, social media is a learned habit. Every company needs to find its own rhythm and pace. But whatever they are, it is important to stick to them in order to build a following and to meet the expectations of your audience. It's not helpful when a company blogs, tweets, or posts to Facebook every other month. That's no way to build a following.

Every company needs to create and develop its own philosophy for engaging with social media. By following some of these basic tenets, forged over the years by some of the leading online brands, you will stand a greater chance of seeing a positive impact.

Above All Else, Be Creative

If you buy into the importance of social media, then you are willing to craft a plan, choose the right networks, and follow the rules of the social media road. The next step is the most challenging of all: to be creative. Admittedly, this isn't easy. Many companies never manage to get there because their efforts never get off the ground.

The brands that have flourished online have invested a great deal of energy into being creative with how they use these networks. Many companies have learned that simply posting press releases on Facebook, or pictures of their products on Instagram, is not enough. There is so much more you can do if you think about your brand and how to best set it in flight in these online arenas. You're only limited by your creativity. Here are some interesting examples that I have seen:

- **Give Away a T-Shirt**. Chargify, a software company based in Boston, gives away T-shirts to enthusiasts (not just paying customers) and encourages users to post pictures of themselves on social networks wearing them. Results? Happy, grateful fans, and free advertising from the scores who participate.

- **Ask for a Recommendation**. Charis Counseling, a mental health practice, asks followers to recommend books for its reading library. The reaction? Engaged fans who connect with the brand, based upon something important to them.
- **Share a Quote**. The Photographer Within, an online community that trains aspiring photographers, takes inspiring quotes from famous people and crafts them into images, with the community's logo placed in a discrete yet discernible location. The result? Brand association with famous people or sayings, and free exposure when fans share the images with their friends.
- **Tap into Cultural Conventions.** Social media is an opportunity to look at what drives people's social actions (i.e., what caused them to like or share things) and feed their desires. Nabisco capitalized on this notion when it launched the "Momisms" campaign for its Nilla brand of wafers. The campaign invented or repurposed a number of sayings that mothers (i.e., Nilla's target audience) would identify with and want to share with their peers. The core of the campaign consisted of quotes that used the yellow-and-red color scheme of the Nilla Wafers package and were branded with the Nilla logo. Momism examples included the following: "They'll never know it's not from scratch," and "I still fit into the earrings I wore in high school." A peek at the Facebook and Pinterest pages for

Momisms shows all sorts of likes, comments, and shares. Talk about brilliant! Kudos to Gary Vaynerchuk for the campaign idea.

- **Enlist Others to Help**. Bolthouse Farms, makers of specialty juice blends, engaged (presumably for a fee) well-known photographers on Instagram to take pictures of their products in interesting settings and share them with their followers. Since many of these photographers already had large followings, the exposure to the brand was massive. Bolthouse also implemented a hashtag to encourage consumers to share, participate, and sign up for a discount.

- **Be Silly**. Chiquita Banana, who has a long-standing and fun brand reputation, created a blue sticker for its bananas that said, "Place Sticker on Forehead. Smile. Chiquita." You can imagine what happened: countless people posting pictures of themselves online, smiling, with the company logo directly on their foreheads.

- **Ask a Trivia Question**. This is not very hard for brands to do, but asking a trivia question to your audience is a great way to get them to respond. If you can associate it with your brand, that's even better.

- **Run a Contest**. Ask users to do something on Instagram or Twitter, and choose a winner. The Cincinnati Reds, a Major League Baseball team, frequently asks fans to post pictures of themselves in Reds gear or in the stadium, with a particular hashtag. The flood of photos helps the team to have fans remind other fans of upcoming games or team events.

- **Be Timely**. Watch out for interesting or widespread events that create unique opportunities for your brand. Oreo Cookie was widely praised after a recent Super Bowl when it came up with a fun online post after the lights went out in the stadium and play was stalled for thirty-four minutes. The ad simply said, "You Can Still Dunk in the Dark"—placed right next to a cookie. The result? Tens of thousands of retweets, and twenty thousand new likes on Facebook. It has also been described as one of the Ten Greatest Tweets of All Time. All because someone (who happened to be quite creative) was paying attention and was willing to act quickly.

We could go on and on with examples, but hopefully the message is clear: creativity, ingenuity, and inventiveness drive engagement. What's more, all of these examples thrived and flourished without ever overtly selling anything. And that's Content Marketing 101.

In order to get people's attention and get them involved, you have to expand your horizons creatively to begin thinking about what's possible and what's original. Unfortunately, there's no formula for this type of approach, but hopefully you can learn from those who have been there and done that.

The Four Gears Working Together

Like the fourth gear in a digital marketing machine, social media plays a critical role. But social media flourishes only when (1) we truly understand our audience; (2) we create original content, distributed through our blog, in forms that are relevant to that audience; and (3) we take a methodical approach to search marketing. The diagram below is a visual model of how the four activities work together:

The four activities within the four-step digital marketing model should be viewed as interdependent gears that work together like the innards of a machine. When one gear stops functioning, the entire machine does.

When those four gears are working together, good things can happen. You create good content for an audience that wants it, the content gets shared and promoted on social media, and Google rewards you with positive search rankings. Looking at the four gears in a different way, high search rankings acquired from great content are likely to create more social sharing from one member of a specific audience to another.

That said, when one gear fails to operate properly, it can disrupt the performance of the entire machine. Great content for the wrong audience will rarely be *Found* on Google because the people searching for it are not the ones buying your product. As another example, great content without social engagement will seldom be *Found* by your audience because the lack of social signals will be penalized by Google and others.

We can go on and on with hypotheticals, but hopefully by now the statistics, stories, and anecdotes will help you understand what my nearly twenty years of experience has taught me: the four gears need to be working in concert in order to function well and produce momentum.

PART 3:
GETTING IT DONE

An ounce of action is worth a ton of theory.

—Ralph Waldo Emerson

Undoubtedly, implementing the ideas and methods described in this book requires a great deal of focus. It is no small task to get your arms around these ideas and methods. The final section of this book looks at some ways you can get started with putting them into action, and how to deal with the barriers and hurdles you may encounter. One of the more common barriers is a lack of time and/or resources to do these things. As such, this section finishes with a chapter dedicated to some free or inexpensive software tools that can help you get organized and on the right track. If you accept the arguments in this book about how the landscape has changed, moving forward may be a matter of survival to your organization. At the very least, implementing these ideas represent a real chance to outmaneuver your competitors.

LIGHTING A FIRE AT YOUR COMPANY

> *The greatest danger in times of turbulence is not the turbulence; it is to act with yesterday's logic.*
>
> —Peter Drucker

Starting Your Company's Engines

Thus far in the book, we have made two points: (1) changes in technology have changed the consumer marketing landscape, and (2) connecting with that consumer requires that marketers do four things well in order to be competitive in the future. The primary question to ask yourself is whether you accept the validity of the first of these two points. Once you do, the next issue to ponder is how your company, on the whole, can follow through on the second.

When it comes to your company, this is probably a difficult question to answer. And it becomes more complex based upon the size of your company, its culture, and what *your* position is within it. If you are an upcoming marketing assistant inside a company of five hundred people or the owner of a hundred-person small business, your ability to impact your situation will vary. In either case, though, everyone has a stake in the success of their organization and should contemplate ways to make an impact.

Some companies may look at the precepts of this book and perhaps need a little fine-tuning or some acceleration of a particular effort. In other situations, companies may be completely dead in the water with respect to these ideas. It has been my experience, though, that all companies (including mine) can improve in at least one, if not all, of the activities represented by the four gears.

In order to help this process along, there is one fundamental step: someone's will to see a change. Whether you are the CEO or a CSR, you can have an impact. This will—this inner resolve to see change—really starts the fire within a company. It starts with this choice and, if given time, it can create real and lasting change.

Companies must simply make the decision to spark real and lasting change.

A Culture Shift

If you use a simple working definition of organizational culture as "the way we do things here," you realize that a culture simply must change in order to adopt these principles and move ahead. Since many of these concepts will be new to most companies, by default, "the way we do things here" will have to shift to "the way we *used* to do things here." Certainly, some companies have always been good about adopting new technologies. But remember, it's not just about technology—it's about how (and where) we relate to customers. It's also about shifting from a reliance on "salesy" advertising to a belief in influential content.

Culture shifts don't happen overnight. They often take months or years at best. But a few simple steps can help you create an impact on the way your company thinks about these issues. In my experience with companies that want to wrestle with these issues, here are a few things that I have seen that got the attention of the organization:
- Sharing statistics
- Highlighting competitor tactics
- Asking challenging questions
- Sharing relevant articles
- Having a "lunch-and-learn" seminar

- Sharing notes from a webinar
- Hosting an expert speaker

Assuming that one or more of these tactics get the attention of those within the organization, any number of small steps can lead to big changes.

Starting Small

Once the organization agrees to move forward, there is no single way that progress must take shape. The most important idea is to begin with small steps that serve as foundational elements for new habits within the organization. These become examples for the way the organization does things *now*. The organization's culture (i.e., "the way we do things here") now includes things such as Facebook updates and blog posts.

Once the organization embraces these new cultural norms, the sky is the limit. But what should these first steps look like? Each organization's initial steps will look different depending upon its size and situation, but here are some initial ideas for the first steps that an organization might take:

- Draft a social media policy document that outlines the ways in which the organization's employees will conduct themselves online.
- Develop a brief plan for a company blog, publishing schedule, and some initial posts.
- Secure company accounts on selected social networks like Twitter, Facebook, and Google+.

These tactics are small but visible ways to signal that the organization is making changes in the way it does business—and that it intends to embrace opportunities to connect with customers in the "always on" world.

Assembling Your Team

Once your organization begins to see small steps take hold, it is critical to assess the skills within your organization with respect to those required for success. Whether the organization has three people or three thousand, certain skills are required to achieve digital marketing success.

The critical skills required vary in both area and degree. The key skills that serve as the foundation of the organization are (a) graphic design, (b) social media, (c) search engine optimization, and (d) writing. Graphic design skills are required for creating and editing images, photographs, and diagrams. Social media skills are necessary for navigating the different social networks and posting, responding, and monitoring their transactions. Search engine skills are required for understanding how to effectively manage all of the search requirements necessary to be *Found* on Google and Bing. And writing skills are necessary, of course, to create written content for your blog and social networks.

It is possible that some individuals have more than one of these skills in their toolboxes. Some highly skilled writers, for example, have developed a strong ability to work well with search engines. But it is very rare for one person within an organization to have all of these skills. And even if someone does, it is likely that their level of sophistication in those skills will vary.

Ideally, an organization should have these key skills in varying degrees. Each of these skills should be present in various levels in order for success to be assured. These skills should be present in at least two levels: (a) strategic and (b) tactical. Strategic skill is required in order to provide a layer of alignment, sophistication, and context to all of the digital marketing activities to be performed within the organization. Tactical skill actually performs the day-to-day activities required, and brings energy and life to executing the strategy.

It is easier to visualize the spectrum of skills by placing them in the matrix below. The matrix shows the many skills required, as well as the degrees that go along with the skills themselves.

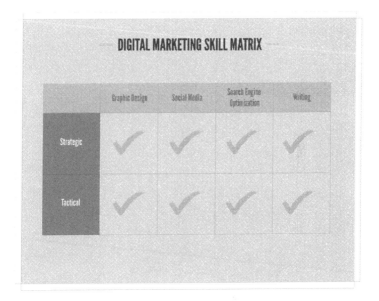

To be *Found*, it is critical for an organization to visualize and
fulfill skill requirements, in both diversity and degree.

The reasons why different degrees of skill are important are many. Primarily, though, it is important to recognize that having tactical skill in your organization is not enough to be successful. An individual on your team may be well versed in using social media accounts on a personal level, but may have little or no understanding of how his or her activities fit into the broader strategic efforts that the company is making. That person might be able to post an update on Twitter, but will have no idea how to reach the proper audience with the messaging, or how to integrate it with the search engine strategy being implemented. If a company relies on tactical skill alone, the end result of its digital marketing efforts can be minimal or nonexistent.

To understand this more explicitly, let's take a look at the skill matrix once again, but with labels on each of the locations within the matrix to demonstrate some practical examples.

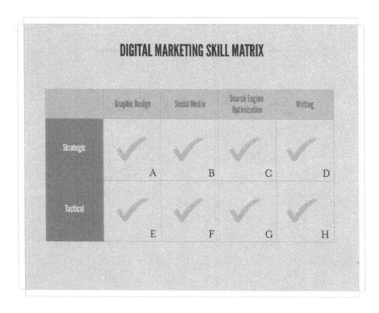

The Digital Marketing Skill Matrix with designated position indicators.

When I speak to many companies and ask them about internal resources for social media, they instinctively say, "We already have that area covered." They might go on to say that they have a "social media wiz" who is on Pinterest all the time. When I do a little digging, what they really mean is that they have someone with tactical skill (location F) in the area, but a severe void in strategic and supervisory degrees of that skill. In other instances, I've spoken to marketing executives who have a great grasp of the strategic side of social media (location B) but little time or patience for the tactical requirements of that function on a day-to-day basis.

When your organization faces a void in these skill areas, there are a variety of ways to compensate. For starters, you can train existing team members in these skill areas. You might also hire new team members who have these skills. Digital marketing skills should be viewed as a big "plus" for any new hires the organization might be making. As a third option, consider engaging a consultant or agency to augment your skills or resources.

Encountering Organizational Barriers

Along the way, it is not uncommon for these ideas or initial steps to meet with some resistance. In fact, it is likely that you will encounter such resistance. A recent study by Weber Shandwick revealed that a mere 18 percent of CEOs have at least one social networking account.

> Only eighteen percent of CEOs have at least one
> social networking account.
>
> --Weber Shandwick

Said another way, four out of five CEOs have no social media presence. While this will likely change in the coming years, it serves to demonstrate that there is little support, interest, or understanding among CEOs.

> Ultimately, [CEOs have] to embrace social, not just
> wave the red flag. They have to live it.
>
> --Charlene Li, Founder, Altimeter Group

Most often, the resulting barriers come from a place of either ignorance or personal bias against these technologies. This is a point to contemplate, especially if you want to build organizational momentum from the top down. In the words of Altimeter Group founder Charlene Li, "ultimately [CEOs have] to embrace social, not just wave the red flag. They have to live it."

Over the years I have heard many executives express resistance to digital marketing tactics in what have become familiar refrains. While they have spoken quite clearly about their opinions and feelings, I have come to detect hidden meanings in their statements. What they say and what they mean are two different things. Some of the examples are included in the table below:

Digital Marketing Denial	
What an executive says	**What an executive often means**
We already have someone here who is great with social media.	Our company has an employee who is active in social media in her personal life, but has no experience with strategic social media.
We have our keywords in our site already.	We once had a meeting to discuss search engine optimization, but we never really fully developed or executed a plan.
We are already on Twitter and Facebook.	Our company has created some social media accounts, but we don't have a strategy or consistent activity.
We already have a blog.	I don't believe in blogs and we haven't updated ours in six months.
Our customers don't buy from us on our website.	I haven't really thought through the way our customers use our website as part of their buying process.

When you encounter these barriers, I have found that there are many avenues that individuals can take to overcome them. If you show some persistence and patience, here are some tactics to advance the digital marketing cause within an organization:

- **Share facts and figures.** There are profound statistics about the impact of digital marketing being developed and shared on a daily basis. Sharing ideas as facts—not opinions—can help to buttress your argument.
- **Circulate competitor tactics.** There is nothing quite as motivating to an organization as the movements of its competitors. Keep an eye on your competitors and their progress with social media tactics, and share the information with naysayers.
- **Share articles from well-known or traditional publications.** When a well-known columnist or publication publishes an article on digital marketing trends, share it with others in your organization. The fact that it comes from a mainstream or traditional source—not a new media advocate—can help the argument create more internal momentum.
- **Enlist other advocates within your organization.** It is well known that there is safety (and strength) in numbers. Identify like-minded digital marketing advocates in your organization, and seek to drum up collective support for these ideas by getting them in the same room to talk about these issues. If it is in front of company leadership, that's all the better.
- **Share stories about Jane.** As trite as it sounds, it is helpful to share anecdotes about your customers

and how they have changed their behavior in the age of "always on." Point to their use of an iPad in a meeting, their use of Facebook in finding a babysitter, or their rants on LinkedIn. If you continue to make the case that your customers are active recipients of digital marketing tactics, there's a good chance that your company's leadership will want to be on the delivery end.

Over time, it is quite possible for real change to take place, especially if you take small steps. I have seen companies shift their attitudes and cultures through the sharing of information and anecdotes. Once a company agrees to take a small step or two, the culture can truly change, and digital marketing tactics can become a part of "how we do things here."

Clara Shigh, CEO of Hearsay Social (an enterprise social media software company), encourages firms to move forward under a three-step framework:

(1) enabling and training employees to effectively use social media for business;

(2) creating social business programs and guidelines;

(3) applying key business metrics to turn grand visions of social media into real business processes and return on investment (ROI).

TOOLS OF THE TRADE

A determined soul will do more with a rusty monkey wrench than a loafer will accomplish with all the tools in a machine shop.

—Robert Hughes

Tools to Aid Your Success

In this book we have described several models, methodologies, and matrixes to help you connect with customers in the age of "always on." Admittedly, success involves a great number of things to think about, moving parts, new technologies, and things to remember. Thankfully, though, you don't have to do it all alone.

There are a great number of tools available to assist you in your work. These tools can help you and your team divide the labor, keep yourselves on a schedule, and even automate a number of the tasks involved, in your quest for success.

In this final chapter of the book I want to share a number of these tools with you. These tools will keep you organized, focused, and locked in on creating and nurturing new customer relationships. The nice thing about this list of tools is that many of them are either free or very inexpensive.

> If you can't measure it, you can't manage it.
> --Peter Drucker

On the whole, this list of tools will help you have a great impact, at little or no cost. For your convenience I have sorted them into some practical groups. Some of these tools might fit into multiple groups, but I have done my best to list them in the most appropriate places. These tools (and others) can also be found at www.FoundTheBook.com in the "Resources" section.

Tools to Help You Publish Content

As you will recall, much of the success required in being *Found* by customers comes from publishing written content in the form of a blog. There are many tools to help you do just that. Here are some of the ones that we recommend:

- **WordPress**: WordPress is one of the most important tools that any digital marketer can use. It is a blogging platform that can run your entire website, or just your blog. WordPress makes the process of publishing new content very easy for people within your organization. WordPress also features thousands of "plug-ins"—the equivalent of apps for your blog—that allow you to customize your site in a great number of ways. WordPress is free and can be downloaded at www.WordPress.org/download. Remember, it is much better to install your blog *within* your website (i.e., www.yourcompany.com/blog), rather than at a blogging service outside of your website (i.e., www.blogger.com/yourcompany).

- **Editorial Calendar for WordPress**: Editorial Calendar is a WordPress plug-in (or app) that helps you manage the posts for your WordPress blog in a calendar view. This free tool gives you a bird's-eye view of the posts you and the team have in the queue, and when they will be released publicly. The tool also allows you to drag and drop posts from one day to another, and to edit posts on the fly. This plug-in can be downloaded at www.WordPress.org/plugins/editorial-calendar.

- **Google Drive**: Google Drive (formerly Google Docs) helps you create lists, calendars, and content for your team to view, edit, and develop. With Google Drive, you can create online documents and spreadsheets and share them with others, who can edit them with you. It is a great tool for drafting blog posts, content calendars, or brainstorming. Google Drive is available for free at www.google.com/drive.

- **HubSpot Blog Topic Generator**: Struggling with the task of coming up with relevant blog post topics? HubSpot has created a helpful tool that turns keywords into blog post headlines. You can enter three nouns and the site will produce a handful of topics that you can use as blog post starters. You can use the tool for free at www.hubspot.com/blog-topic-generator .

- **Evernote**: Evernote is a lifesaver for creating and sharing notes, lists, pictures, and virtually anything else you can think of. It's a great brainstorming and collaboration tool that can be used from a computer, smartphone, or tablet. You can create separate notebooks and tags that can be shared with others, and you can add ideas on the fly. When it is time to write new blog posts, your ideas will be there in Evernote for you. Evernote offers both free and inexpensive paid versions at www.evernote.com. Its apps are available for free in the Apple and Android app stores.

- **Hemingway**: The Hemingway app (www. hemingwayapp.com) helps turn your lengthy prose into clear language that is simpler for readers. You can paste your blog posts into the app and receive instant feedback on flowery language, word choice, and voice.

Social Media Tools

Once you start churning out blog posts, there are a number of tools available to help you share them online, engage users, and monitor what customers are saying about your brand and competitors. Here are some helpful tools for you to experiment with:

- **HootSuite**: HootSuite is a tool that, among other things, helps you manage multiple Twitter accounts and to preschedule posts on various social networks. It offers free and paid versions at www.hootsuite.com.
- **TweetDeck**: TweetDeck, which is owned by Twitter, is similar to HootSuite but is particularly helpful for monitoring Twitter for mentions of your brand, industry, or keywords that might signal a parachute moment for you. It can be accessed at www.tweetdeck.com.

- **Bitly**: Once you start sharing links online, it is important to shorten them and monitor their performance. Bitly (www.bitly.com) is a tool that helps you do just that. You can track how many times a link is accessed, in one convenient dashboard.

- **FollowerWonk**: FollowerWonk is a tool that lets you dive deeply into your Twitter accounts and identify trends and users that can help you amplify your message. It offers free and paid editions and has some powerful reporting features at www.followerwonk.com.

- **Hashtags.org**: This is a site that allows you to identify and utilize hashtags that are popular or trending. If you aren't familiar with them, hashtags are words with the "#" symbol in front of them that allow users to communicate and connect around a topic, event, or concept. For example, entrepreneurs may include *#startup* within their tweet to connect with others who may also be using or viewing this term. Not surprisingly, the site's URL is www.hashtags.org.

- **TweetAdder**: This tool helps you zoom in on Twitter users who are connected to your brand's topics. It helps you to monitor follower activity and identify users who can help you grow your following and social reach. The tool is online at www.tweetadder.com.

- **JustReTweet**: This site is a community of users that encourages members to retweet relevant content from one another. While some users may use a tool like this gratuitously, it may be helpful for you to connect with fellow Twitter account owners anxious to share *your* message with *their* followers. You can sign up at www.justretweet. com.

Tools to Help You Gain Search Visitors

Along with tools for social sharing, there are a number of tools that can help you connect with search engines such as Google and Bing. Spending some time learning about and using these tools can help you to position yourself to rank highly in search results when users search for your product or service.

- **Google Keyword Planner**: Google offers a free tool within its Adwords product that allows you to search its database of search queries to see what words are used most often when users are searching for your product. If you are marketing fresh fruit, for example, this tool can help you determine how often users are searching for "organic fruit" versus "local produce." Experiment with a few examples at http://adwords.google. com/ko/KeywordPlanner/Home.
- **Wordtracker**: Wordtracker is a more focused, intensive version of Google Keyword Planner.

It is an established, highly respected keyword research tool, and it's available for a nominal monthly subscription fee. You can try some free queries and sign up at www.wordtracker.com.

- **Raven:** Raven is a comprehensive marketing platform with some powerful search engine marketing tools. It is very complex and worth the investment. It can be accessed at www.raventools.com.

- **WordPress SEO by Yoast:** This plug-in can be installed within WordPress to ensure that your blog posts are optimized for the proper keywords. The plug-in guides your writing and can alert you when your keywords are not properly placed in your post titles, body copy, or elsewhere. It can be freely downloaded at www.yoast.com/WordPress/seo.

Tools for Measuring Results

Peter Drucker is famous for saying, "If you can't measure it, you can't manage it." With all the investments of time and other resources you decide to make in digital marketing, it is important to keep tabs on what is working, what is not, and how your efforts are generating a return for your labor. The following tools can help you do just that.

- **Google Analytics:** This free tool is a must for digital marketers. Offered by Google, it is a metrics tool that you can install on your website.

Google Analytics gauges the activity within your site. It can tell you where and how your web visitors found your site, where they came from, how long they stayed, and what pages they viewed—among several hundred other factors. There are many other analytics tools available, but this one is highly recommended, compatible with many other services, and simple to understand. It can be downloaded and installed at www.google.com/analytics.

- **Visual.ly Google Analytics Report:** Visual.ly offers a great service to help you visualize your analytics results on an ongoing basis. With all of the data that Google Analytics offers, this tool can help you digest some of its more important facets. You can sign up for free at www.visual.ly/google-analytics-report.

- **Ducksboard:** Ducksboard is a dashboard product that can help you put many of these metrics on a screen that can be monitored publicly by your team on a computer screen, mobile device, or flat-screen television. It is affordable and a free trial is available at www.ducksboard.com.

- **Statigram:** Statigram is a platform-specific site that helps you monitor your brand's Instagram activity. It can show you how popular your account's posts are and how your followers are growing. It can also provide a geographical distribution of their locations. It is available for free at www.statigr.am.

- **Klout:** Klout is a tool that helps you understand your social influence by assigning each account a Klout score. Klout rates users using proprietary formulas and helps you track progress. It works with accounts on Twitter, Facebook, Google+, and many more. Try it for free at www.klout.com.

JOIN THE CONVERSATION

As you read this book, you are invited to share your thoughts and ideas in a number of ways. Here are a few opportunities to do so:

- Visit www.FoundTheBook.com for links to resources, learning opportunities, and more.
- For free Findsome & Winmore gear, write a review of the book on Amazon.com and e-mail your mailing address to info@findsomewinmore.com with a link to your review.
- E-mail your feedback and comments to the author: mcerto@findsomewinmore.com.
- Use the #FoundBook hashtag to share your thoughts and ideas on the book.

Made in the USA
Charleston, SC
14 May 2014